anyike
okpoka @hotmail.co

Safeguarding

Your

Home

© 2006 A.D - **SAFEGUARDING YOUR HOME**
Dr. D.K. Olukoya
ISBN: 978-8021-70 -0
A Publication of
TRACTS AND PUBLICATIONS GROUP
MOUNTAIN OF FIRE AND MIRACLES MINISTRIES
13, Olasimbo Street, off Olumo Road, (By UNILAG Second
Gate), Onike, Iwaya.
P.O.Box 2990, Sabo, Yaba, Lagos, Nigeria. 01-867439,
4704267,4704367
Website: www.mountain-of-fire.com
E-mail: mfmhqworldwide@mountainoffire.org

First Edition

i

TABLE OF CONTENTS

INTRODUCTION

Many Christians are suffering from spiritual diabetes; that is, there is too much sugar in their spiritual blood. They want to see heavenly revelations like Jacob, but have forgotten that before Jacob could see heavenly visions, he was alone with God and his pillow was a stone. Christians today, prefer to sleep on comfortable mattresses and pillows, not on stones like Jacob. They want to sleep on the lap of 'Delilah' and wake up on the bosom of Abraham. Many know that certain things are against the will of God, but go ahead and do them. Many see nothing, hear nothing and are constantly falling into the pit of spiritual darkness. Many are unable to retain what they hear or read from the word of God. This is actually the crux of the matter discussed in this book and I would advise that you take every bit of it seriously.

Marriage is an institution that was ordained by God in the Garden of Eden. Man and woman were at peace with God until the serpent came in to tempt them and they fell. They lost the glory of God upon their lives and covered themselves with fig leaves. Today, many homes have lost the glory of God and are covering up with attitudes, religion, infidelity, polygamy and all sorts of things that the devil brings their way.

Many Christians do not realise the kind of warfare that they are involved in and so, they either do not fight and the enemy destroys them, or they do not use the right weapons and the enemy destroys them still.

Some people are aware of the spiritual battle that is going on against the home, but have doors that they left open, which have served as entry points to the enemy. The devil is taking advantage of the ignorance of so many Christians and is cheating them steadily. Many people are sharing their spouses with different things: some share their husbands or wives with work; others share their spouses with a hobby, parents, friends, lovers, or strange men and women.

In this book, we shall highlight the factors that favour the enemy against Christian homes. Some of these things have been in existence before some people were born and that takes into account the need for deliverance. We shall also show how homes can be guarded, so that the enemy will no longer gain entrance into the marital lives of the children of God. Read and digest and allow the Lord to minister to you and meet you at the very point of your need.

CHAPTER ONE
THE UNPROFITABLE LEAKAGE

Matthew 13:3-8: *"And He spake many things unto them in parables, saying, Behold, a sower went forth to sow; and when he sowed, some seeds fell by the way side, and the fowls came and devoured them up: Some fell upon stony places, where they had not much earth: and forthwith they sprung up, because they had no deepness of earth: and when the sun was up, they were scorched; and because they had no root, they withered away. And some fell among thorns; and the thorns sprung up, and choked them: but others fell into good ground and brought forth fruit, some an hundredfold, some sixtyfold, some thirtyfold."*

Matthew 13:13: *"Therefore speak I to them in parables: because they seeing see not; and hearing they hear not, neither do they understand."*

Matthew 13:18-23: *"Hear ye therefore the parable of the sower. When any one heareth the word of the kingdom, and understandeth it not, then cometh the wicked one, and catcheth away that which was sown in his heart. This is he which received seed by the way side. But he that received the seed into stony places, the same is he that heareth the word, and anon with joy receiveth it; Yet hath he not root in himself, but dureth for a while: for when tribulation or persecution ariseth because of the word, by and by he is offended. He also that received seed among the thorns is he that heareth the word; and the care of this world, and the deceitfulness of riches, choke the word, and he becometh unfruitful. But he that received seed into the good ground is he that heareth the word, and understandeth it; which also beareth fruit, and bringeth forth, some an hundredfold, some sixty, some thirty."*

This parable talks about four places:
1. Road-side.
2. Stony ground.
3. Among thorns.
4. Good ground.

These four places represent four types of people, hearers of the word of God, and four types of people who want things from God.

Note the following points about this parable:

The sower was not a bad man. He had no problem. The seeds too were good; the problem came from the type of ground on which the seeds fell. The problem is not that people do not receive blessings from God; the problem is that the blessings leak out. That is spiritual leakage. At such times, even praying becomes difficult nd almost of no effect. Many people who are praying or financial breakthroughs need to first pray that the piritual holes in their pockets be sealed so that when hey put anything in it, it will not fall off. Many people come to God for water with a basket. Some actually had buckets but the enemy stole them from them. When God sees that it is a basket, He will not pour water in it. Until the holes through which the blessings are siphoned become sealed, the blessings of some people will not be a reality. They will see it, feel it, but will not have it. The case of such people will be like that of the fisherman who caught a fish and the fish managed to wriggle its way back into the river. It would be painful because he would have wasted the worms that he used as bait to catch it.

There was a sister who was frantically seeking employment and I told her that her problem was not a job but that she needed to pray to seal the spiritual holes in her pocket. She did not agree with me and so did not pray the prayers. Soon afterwards, she got a job as shop attendant in a supermarket. She had a manager who always suspected the attendants of stealing and would deduct the price of anything that got missing from their salaries. The very month she started work, things got missing and automatically, the cost was deducted from her salary. At the end of the month, her take-home pay was less than the price of a bowl of rice whereas, she had borrowed money from people to buy new dresses for her work and also to pay her transport fare for that month with the hope of paying back when she received her salary. She stayed on thinking that it was because it was the first month, that by the following month, she would have understood the place better. At the end of the second month, the same thing happened and she came back to me and I reminded her of her leaking pockets.

If you find that you are working and there is nothing to show for it, everything is being swallowed up by forces that you cannot see; it means your pockets are leaking spiritually. Victims of leaking pockets would receive money but would not know how the money was spent. They would work so hard, but there would be little or no financial gain. They would get jobs, but they would slip off their hands. They would go for interviews and it would be confirmed that they were the best, but for no obvious reason, they would not be employed. They are those who would get to a place of interview and their dressing or looks would put the interviewers off. The interviewers would promise to get in touch with them but they would never hear from them. When customers are avoiding your shop and are going to new ones, it means that there is something wrong somewhere.

If you discover that anytime you make any financial gain, problems would mount and swallow up the money or that when you have money, members of your family would take ill one after the other and the money that was meant to enhance your business or improve your general well-being, would be spent on drugs, then there is a problem. The situation could be so bad that you are plunged into a heavy debt that would be settled as soon as you get another large sum of money. It is not that people who are affected are not praying; they are, but they have not really hit the target.

When a person finds it difficult to keep a regular job, or experiences unexplainable loss of money, it means that there is a leakage somewhere. Such people have problematic health that would require expensive drugs and terrible, major, surgical interventions that would gulp a lot of money. Such people would have financial handicap, in spite of reasonable income. When a person is always cheated or duped or is always a victim of theft, there is a spiritual leakage somewhere.

It is also possible for a person to experience spiritual leakage in his or her spiritual life. The person would remember that he or she used to speak in tongues, but now he or she does not. Or that he or she used to be on fire for the Lord, but today has turned very cold or that the person used to prophesy but today, he or she neither sees nor hears anything. Some people used to see visions before they got married, but now they do not see anything. Some used to go about witnessing but now they have lost the zeal. Some people who used to find it difficult to condone sin, are now tolerating it in many ways. Such people are on fire today and are cold tomorrow; all the bad dreams are now coming back; the spiritual problems of the past are resurfacing. They find it difficult to read or memorise the Bible. They try to fast but in the night, they see themselves eating in the dream.

When a person is not improving spiritually, or cannot come out fully for the Lord, it is evidence that he or she is going through a spiritual leakage. When a believer is constantly failing examinations, it means that the person's 'bucket of blessing' is leaking. He or she would always be late to important meetings, experience memory failure and would not be able to maintain a good thing for a long time. Good opportunities slip off their hands; that is why some sisters do not have a settled home. Their husbands will go one way, and they will go another. They hardly talk to each other. In such homes, when a breakthrough is around the corner, husband and wife will start to quarrel and the devil will make sure they do not get that breakthrough. Some die just at the verge of their miracle. Some people get marriage proposals but the suitors back out for strange reasons. All these are evidence of leakage and that must be sealed before it is too late.

Leakage differs from one person to the other in size and intensity. Some can be sealed easily, while some would require more effort. Some people would need to drop their baskets and pick up buckets for their blessings. Sometimes, during such leakages, God reveals through dreams and visions that something is wrong somewhere. Most times, such people do not understand or do not even know that God is trying to show them anything. Sometime ago, a certain woman came to tell me that her husband locked himself up in a room, and did not want to see her. This man lived abroad for twenty-four years. The room had a bath and toilet, so he had his bath there. I asked how he was feeding and she said that she would put his food by the door and when he was sure nobody was looking, he would open the door and take the food in. I told her it was a spiritual problem and that the devil was trying to ruin her marriage. She told me that long ago, she had a dream where someone took her wedding dress and hit it with a hammer. I told her that that was the day the devil got hold of her marriage. I told her that she had to summon the person that hit the wedding gown with a hammer and revoke what the person did. Also, I told her that things would change if prayer warriors started praying in that house. She did not believe me until she saw the raw power of God at work. Spiritual leakage kills easily.

Job 33:15-18 says, *"In a dream, in a vision of the night, when deep sleep falleth upon men, in slumberings upon the bed; then he openeth the ears of men, and sealeth their instruction. That he may withdraw man from his purpose, and hide pride from man. He keepeth back his soul from the pit and his life from perishing by the sword."*

Sometimes, God speaks through dreams and visions in order to warn His children. That is why we should not take our dreams for granted, no matter how spiritual we are. Every dream that is coming regularly should be treated with all seriousness; it could be a pointer to where you should direct your prayers. When a person is having spiritual leakage, he could see himself in a dream where he is being given something good like a baby or money or a parcel and then another person comes along and orders him to hand over the thing and he complies. Such people have to pray hard and recover what has been forcefully taken from them. If you find yourself spending money lavishly or in a party and you are 'spraying' money on people that are dancing, it means there is a leakage and you have to recall that party and recover your money from the people that you sprayed. If you find yourself counting coins, it is a sign of leakage. It is even worse if the number of coins you counted is five. It means there is a monetary problem somewhere.

A certain man said that anytime his pay-day was approaching, he would see himself in the market buying things. He did not know that it was leakage, until he started praying seriously. If you see that you put something in your pocket in the dream and it dropped, or that you lost a huge amount of money in the dream, you should know that there is a leakage somewhere. If you find yourself looking at your property being auctioned by someone else, it is leakage. If you find yourself in the dream, searching for something and you never found it or you were climbing an unending staircase, or you see yourself plucking rotten or unripe fruits, or that you are in a market buying second-hand clothes, it means that God is trying to tell you that there is problem lurking somewhere. If you see yourself in a dream where someone punched a hole in an organ in your body, or that you went blind, you have to really pray hard. If you see yourself being pursued by dangerous animals or giant creatures, and masquerades, or you see yourself being buried or you find your name on the list of those who failed an examination. you have to really pray hard.

If you have ever nad any of these dreams, you have to pray, recall and cancel them. These are the kinds of things that the Bible describes as wells without water, or clouds without rain. All the powers that cause spiritual leakage do not hinder people from accumulating things but they wait until the things have been accumulated and then they would come and waste it. The powers of spiritual leakage make people see things but will not allow them to enjoy them; or they behold but do not appropriate.

2 Kings 7:1-2 says, *"Then Elisha said, Hear ye the word of the Lord; thus saith the Lord: Tomorrow about this time shall a measure of fine flour be sold for a shekel and two measures of barley for a shekel, in the gate of Samaria" Then a lord on whose hand the king leaned answered the man of God, and said: Behold, if the Lord would make windows in heaven, might this thing be? And he said: Behold, thou shalt see it with thine eyes, but shalt not eat thereof."*

2 Kings 7:18-20: *"And it came to pass as the man of God had spoken to the king, saying: Two measures of barley for a shekel, and a measure of fine flour for a shekel, shall be to morrow about this time in the gate of Samaria. And that lord answered the man of God, and said: Now, behold, if the Lord should make windows in heaven, might such a thing be? And he said: Behold, thou shalt see it with thine eyes, but shalt not eat thereof. And so it fell out unto him: for the people trode upon him in the gate, and he died."* The powers of leakage made the man in this text to see what God said He would do, but he did not enjoy it. His mouth was the instrument of his destruction.

Spiritual leakage leads to disappointment and frustration. A person cannot be a blessing if he himself is not blessed. The only person that can stop God's plan for your life is you; not your enemy or anyone else.

That is why there is a difference between a good idea and a God-inspired idea. A good idea is not necessarily a God-sanctioned idea. The powers of spiritual leakage will give a good idea, which might be contrary to God's will for you. You are likely to embrace a thing because it is good but that does not mean that God wants it for you. The thing might be correct or logical but not right. The Bible says a man shall receive nothing except it is given him from above. It means that those things that people receive from below are not right for them. God will necessarily have to withdraw those things which are from below from you, before He gives you His own. That is why, when some people give their lives to Christ, they become poor. It is because God wants to purge their lives of the wealth that they acquired from the table of the devil. Later, God will give them His own wealth. He will then bless them with His own blessings which has no sorrow. People who receive money, property, future partner, etc from below, and stick to them have not received from the Lord. This is the number one strategy of the power-sucking spiritual leakage; they make people stick to what they should run away from.

Sometime ago, one of our fathers-in-the-Lord had a vision as he was praying for his congregation. He saw a caterer with a big pot of food and a long queue of people in front of him. The people were wailing and asking him to give them food. Surprisingly, the caterer too was weeping and telling them that he would like to dish out the food but their plates were dirty. He told them to wash their plates before he could give them the food. God ministered to this our father in the Lord, that his congregation that he was praying for had a lot of strange property in their hands and He had no space to put what He wanted to give them.

These powers make people get married to particular sins. Sin is the root of all evil. All manners of evil draw their bitterness from the fountain of sin. It is more dangerous than temptation, trials, sickness, and even death, because it kills twice. Satan cannot harm a child of God, unless he is given the permission through sin. The enemy tries to hide the horrible consequence of sin. What you sow in thoughts, you reap in words. What you sow in words, you reap in actions and what you sow in actions, you will reap in habits. What you sow in habits, you reap in character and what you sow in character, you reap in your destiny, which you might not be comfortable with. All easily besetting sins lead to spiritual leakage. Anyone that is still stealing or telling lies, and is asking God for a life partner is not addressing the issue that he or she should address. When there are anti-marriage forces in your life, God would wait until you have dealt with them before He answers your prayers. If you are seeking financial breakthroughs and you are still proud and are spiritually lukewarm, God would like you to get rid of those things first before He answers your prayers. You might be praying for spiritual breakthroughs but God would want you to deal with the laziness in your life before He answers you.

These powers start a satanic revival at the moment a breakthrough is around the corner. It is when the angel of breakthrough is at the door, that husband and wife would start to quarrel and fight, thereby hindering the angel from delivering his message. It is then that children would kick against their parents. It is at such times that discouragement would set in and prevent a person from attending the prayer meeting where God wants to meet his or her need. It is at such times that someone would come and offend the person. That is when heaviness would set in and there would be intense demonic attacks that could lead to discouragement. God's strategy is to seal up demonic leakages in the lives of His people before filling them up with blessings.

A certain pregnant woman, whose baby had been clinically declared dead, refused to accept the clinical prophecy and to go through an operation to get rid of the dead baby. One day, she attended one of our services and there was a word of knowledge that there was a baby that was being brought back into its mother's womb. Evil powers were taking the baby in and out of the woman's womb. Thank God that the woman knew her God and did not agree to get rid of the baby. She gave birth to a bouncing baby boy on that very day. The powers of leakage were tampering with the baby and his life would have been terminated, if God had not intervened. If you take no action, that would be the end. When some parents get to God, He will line out many offences against them and they will be surprised to know that they had given in to the powers of leakage in the lives of their children.

HOW DOES SPIRITUAL LEAKAGE GET INTO THE LIVES OF PEOPLE?

1. Inheritance: Through parents, ancestors or close relatives. Whenever you notice that an evil spirit or bad behaviour that your father has or had in his life-time is now manifesting in you, you have to start praying immediately. I had a friend who always asked me how I was faring and I would say, "Fine; in Jesus' Name." Whenever I asked him how he was faring, he would say, "The struggle continues until victory or defeat, or both". No wonder he failed his examinations three times. We as believers should know that our victory was won more than two thousand years ago; we are just to enforce it. Many believers are assisting the enemies to fight them hard; they are cooperating with the problems, and are not praying for solution but for the problem. If a demonic influence enters into a family lineage, it goes from generation to generation. Sometimes, when a mother refuses to collect evil powers, the child will collect it. You must refuse to

collect any demonic parcel from any demonic po.
master; tell them that they have come to the wron\
address. Send them back to the senders.

2. **Personal involvement in ungodly activities:**
Belonging to clubs, societies and associations, where
people do not pray but hold discussions on how to
celebrate one thing or the other with a member of the
association or how they will buy one uniform or the
other should be handled with caution because most of
the time, people get initiated into witchcraft through
these kinds of groups. A demonic member could be
given the contract to supply uniforms or head-gears
that they will put on and before distributing it to others
something could done to the uniform or headgear,
which will eventually cause trouble and they will go
about looking for white-garment prophets to bail them
out. The enemy does not put a warning label on his
track so that you do not know when he arrives.

3. **Curses:** These are devil-inspired words uttered by
people against others. Usually, they are meant to harm
or even kill. Such words should be neutralised by the
Blood of Jesus. If anyone utters a negative statement
concerning you and you do not cancel or neutralise it
immediately, it could harm or even kill you but that
does not mean you will not get to heaven. However,
you would not have realised your fullest potentials
because the enemy would have made you stay at the
tail region.

There was a lady who was jilted by her fiancé and she lost her job at the same time. Everything turned upside down for her. Someone advised her to come to our church and she was reluctant because she did not like the way we pray. Finally, she was persuaded and she came for prayers. Brethren rallied round to pray for her and as the prayers were going on, the Lord revealed to a brother, that there was something under the bed of the sister. She was furious and said that was one of the reasons she did not want to come for the prayers. After much persuasion, she agreed to take them to her house. When they got there and looked under the bed, they found a brown paper bag. When it was opened, they found lime, pierced through with needles and two photographs; one of hers and the other was her fiancé's that ran away with another woman. She was stunned. The brethren took the photographs and burnt them and commanded the demons attached to them to go back to the sender. They asked the angels of God to accompany them, so that they would go right back to their sender. Later, the sister discovered that the run-away fiancé was involved in a ghastly motor accident and died with his new woman. When demons are sent back to sender, they become more aggressive. When a person begins to get trouble from all sources and it seems as if the blessing of God cannot stay in the person's life, it means there is a curse hanging over the life of the person.

4. Broken vows: If you break a vow, you are bei
unfaithful. People take this issue lightly, but it is
serious matter. A vow is a solemn promise made to a
person or to God. There is no law forcing people to
make vows, but if you make any, it is compulsory to
fulfill it; especially when you make it to God.

Numbers 30:2 says, *"If a man vow a vow unto the
Lord, or swear an oath to bind his soul with a bond;
he shall not break his word, he shall do according to
all that proceedeth out of his mouth."*

Deuteronomy 23:21 says, *"When thou shalt vow a vow
unto the Lord thy God, thou shalt not slack to pay it:
for the Lord thy God will surely require it of thee;
and it would be sin in thee."*

Proverbs 20:25: *"It is a snare to the man who
devoured that which is holy, and after vows to make
enquiry."*

Ecclesiastes 5:4-5 says, *"When thou vowest a vow
unto God, defer not to pay it; for he hath no
pleasure in fools: pay that which thou hast vowed.
Better is it that thou shouldest not vow, than that
thou shouldest vow and not pay."*

A broken vow can be the source of a big problem. That
was why Jonah had to repent in the belly of the fish

and then redeemed his vow. However, if a vow is discovered to be contrary to the word of God, and will not glorify God, it should be renounced and forgiveness should be sought. A vow that is evil or that is designed for an evil purpose should never be made or kept. If you keep an evil vow because people will think you are inconsistent, then you will be compounding one evil by another. That is why I always feel sorry for those who break marriage vows. Let us examine the vows that people make on their wedding day in the presence of God and man. The priest would charge the man and woman that have decided to come to the altar to be joined together as husband and wife. In the presence of the congregation, the priest would say: "Dearly beloved, as we are gathered here in the presence of God and this congregation to join them together in holy matrimony, which is an honourable estate instituted by God Himself, signifying unto us the union that is between Christ and His church which holy estate Christ adorned and beautified with His presence and His first miracle that He wrought at Cana in Galilee; and is commended in the Holy Scriptures to be honourable among all men and therefore, it is not to be an enterprise, nor taken in hand unavoidably or lightly, but solemnly, discreetly, soberly, in the fear of God. I require and charge you both as you will answer in the dreadful day of judgement when the secret of all hearts shall be disclosed."

It is amazing to find that after pronouncing these dreadful words, some people would wake up one morning and say they are no longer interested in the marriage. They would give one excuse or the other, justifying themselves and condemning their partners complaining about their looks, dressing, age, etc They forget that as soon as they say: "I will", they have made a vow that should not be broken for any reason whatsoever. After making a vow like this before God and before man, woe betides anyone that breaks it. It is better not to get married than to do so and break this kind of vow. It will lead to spiritual leakage in their lives. That is why some men can never make it in life. When a woman would have struggled and sweated to help them survive, they wake up one day and ask the woman to get lost and then, they bring in other women. Even if the women do not say anything, there is an automatic curse that comes into operation as soon as the marriage vow is broken. That was why Jesus told the disciples that it was better not to marry, than to seek divorce. Jesus added that not everybody is able to stay unmarried.

Do not make any vow that you cannot keep. Many people tell God that they will be fasting and praying on certain days, but would have finished taking breakfast, before they remember their vow. Some would promise God that they would work in certain areas in the church but they soon leave it for something else. It is better not to make a vow than to make it and not fulfill it. It results in spiritual leakage. Make today your day of miracles. When God blesses, He blesses to a dumbfounding degree. I do not believe that Christians should be poor in any way; if we have a big God, then we must have big miracles; we do not have to be poor. Today, we have to stand against the forces of spiritual leakage.

Romans 16:20 says, *"And the God of peace shall bruise satan under your feet shortly. The grace of our Lord Jesus Christ be with you. Amen."*

Take the following prayer points with determination in your heart and with the authority of the Lord Jesus Christ in your voice:

1. I close every spiritual hole through which my blessings are leaking out in the name of Jesus.
2. I cancel every unprofitable vow that I have made with anybody, in the name of Jesus.
3. I break every curse of leaking blessings upon my life, in the name of Jesus.
4. Every inherited spirit of leakage in my life, depart from me now, in the name of Jesus.
5. Lord Jesus, lay your hands of power upon me now, in the name of Jesus.
6. Holy Spirit, lay your hands of fire upon my life now, in the name of Jesus.

CHAPTER TWO
TEN TRUTHS THAT THE DEVIL DOES NOT WANT YOU TO KNOW

Psalm 119:89 says, *"For ever, O Lord, Thy word is settled in heaven."*

The word of God is the only unchanging truth. The words of man will change. Most of the science books that were written twenty years ago have been revised or changed. In Nigeria for example, we had story books which were compulsory for pupils learning English, but today, they are no more in circulation. One of such books had the story of 'Abdul and the Angel' and another one had the story of 'Shokolokobangoshe'. Today, they are no longer existent. The syllabus has changed over and over again. The Bible says that God is the Alpha and Omega; that is the 'A' and 'Z'. If you look through the alphabets, you will discover that there are many letters between 'A' and 'Z'.

John 18:37-39 says, *"Pilate therefore said unto him: Art thou a king then? Jesus answered: Thou sayest that I am a king. To this end was I born, and for this cause came I into the world, that I should bear witness unto the truth. Every one that is of the truth heareth my voice. Pilate saith unto Him: What is truth? And when he had said this, he went out again unto the Jews, and saith unto them, I find in him no fault at all."* Pilate did not know the truth. He did not understand the fact that the truth is the word of God. Jesus is the word of God and He is the truth. He was standing before Pilate, but Pilate did not understand Him. Many people are like that today. There was a rich, young man who came to meet the Lord Jesus Christ and asked Him questions on how to get eternal life. Jesus asked him what the Scriptures said and he answered correctly. When Jesus told him to do all that the law demanded, he said he had been doing those things since his youth. Jesus then told him to go and sell his property, distribute to the poor and follow Him. Those conditions were hard for him to follow and the Bible says that the man went away with his head bowed. He was sad. He saw the truth, but did not recognise Him. He was a loser. Although he was far from the truth, he found Him and lost Him. I would like you to pray like this: "O Lord, I do not want to be blind to the truth, I do not want to be just near the truth, I want to be in the truth, in the name of Jesus."

The devil has already been defeated but does not want people to know it. That is why he keeps the truth away from them. The devil also prevents people from using their spiritual weapons and keeps away useful spiritual information. Some people go to gatherings where there is no useful information. Normally, if a gathering is referred to as fellowship of Christians, you should expect at least three things to happen there: you either leave the place mad at yourself, because you have been convicted of your wrongdoings or you leave the place sad, because you have wasted time in the camp of the enemy, or you leave the place happy because you have received solution to your problem or you are glad because you have received salvation, deliverance and healing. If none of these things happen to you, then, it is not a useful gathering.

God has secrets but every thing is open to Him. The devil too has secrets, but the Lord has the power to reveal his secrets to the children of God. Deuteronomy 29:29 says, *"The secret things belong unto the Lord our God: but those things which are revealed belong unto us and to our children for ever, that we may do all the words of this law."*

Daniel 2:22 says, *"He revealeth the deep and secret things: He knoweth what is in the darkness, and the light dwelleth with Him."*

Psalm 25:14 says, *"The secret of the Lord is with them that fear Him; and He will shew them His covenant."* Life has secrets; the devil too has secrets that he does not want the children of God to know. One of the abilities of the devil is the fact that he can remove the word of God from the hearts of people, as we saw in the parable of the sower. Many people can remember worldly songs but cannot remember Bible verses. This is why many churchgoers will find themselves in hell fire; they allow the evil one to remove the fruit of the word of God from their heart. He makes people to be ignorant of what the Bible says about them. He combats useful spiritual information that will move their lives forward. The devil makes people to forget their dreams when they wake up.

TEN TRUTHS THAT THE DEVIL DOES NOT WANT YOU TO KNOW:
1. The devil is a liar: John 8:44-45: *"Ye are of your father the devil, and the lusts of your father ye will do. He was a murderer from the beginning, and abode not in the truth, because there is no truth in him. When he speaketh a lie, he speaketh of his own: for he is a liar and the father of it."*

The devil lied to Adam and Eve and caused them to be chased out of the garden. He came in the form of a serpent and framed a question in a way that Eve got carried away. He knew what God said but asked if God had told them not to eat from the trees of the garden. He told her that they would not die if they ate the fruit of the particular tree which God had commanded them not to eat. He is still using that method on people today; he gives them false security. He makes them believe that they have no problem. In fact, they go to the extent of thinking that it is those who have problems that go to church, so they do not need to go to church.

A sister came to see me one day and I asked what the problem was. She said she had no problem and I asked what she came for. She said she wanted me to pray for her. I asked on what subject and she said: "Generally". I said we do not pray 'General' prayers in MFM but 'Specific' prayers. As we were praying, the Lord revealed the fact that her two legs were a fish tail. There are many people like that today. There are some whom the devil has convinced that they are very intelligent and know more than everybody else. In fact, he would tell them to do what their heart tells them to do. If you listen to the lie of the devil, you will get into trouble.

Pray like this: "I refuse to listen to the lie of the devil, in the name of Jesus."

One night, some prayer warriors were praying and some birds were flying across the church premises. One of the warriors spotted them and pointed at them and one of them crash-landed and turned into an old woman. This was about 2 a. m. The prayer warriors tied her hands and made her sit on the floor and wait till morning. The security men said at a point in time, they were getting weak and were dozing off. At that very moment, the rope with which they tied her was breaking off. When they woke up, they retied the rope. When I got there in the morning, I asked her where she came from and she mentioned the name of her village. I told her that having seen that the power of God is greater than the one she has, would she like to surrender her life to the Lord Jesus Christ? She said 'No', that it was too late, that she had sold her heart and life to the devil. She admitted that the airspace over MFM was not their normal route but they just wanted to try their power that night. Since she was not ready to surrender her life to the Lord Jesus Christ, we asked her to go and she left. It is the devil that tells people lies like this and makes them to stick to evil associations. It is when most of them land in hell that they will know the truth and understand that the devil was deceiving them.

On another occasion, the president and secretary of an evil association were flying over the premises where prayer warriors were praying and the secretary dropped but the president escaped. I pray that the wings of any evil power flying over your habitation shall break and be paralysed, in the Name of Jesus. Beloved, if you are in any evil association such as witchcraft, familiar spirit, etc, you had better renounce it and come to Jesus before it is too late. Do not allow the devil to deceive you with his lies.

One evening, after service a girl said she had a calabash in her stomach. As we were praying for her, she was groaning in pains and started to speak a strange language. We asked her what was the matter and she said that she needed a bucket of water in order to summon mammy water. We got the bucket of water and she chanted some words and later sighed, saying that the spirit could not come into the house, because there was an angel at the door with a sword of fire. That would have been the first time I would have seen mammy water. She was delivered but later, she listened to the lies of the devil who mocked her, that she had become poor and was no longer attractive since she joined Christians.

The devil tells lies everyday just to deceive people. He is the one who tells women that one man is not sufficient for them. He encourages men to take more than one wife; he has his own prophets who imitate the truth, in order to deceive people. He prepares scotch egg for them; the outer coat would be nice and attractive while the inner part would be bad; he knows how to coat lies with some truth; that is why fake prophets tell some truth, so that you would not discover that they are deceiving you.

Lying is an instrument of hypocrisy and deceit. That is why the Bible is harsh on all liars. The Bible says they are of the devil and will find themselves in the lake of fire. It is the lie of the devil to give you a bad picture about your life and tell you that certain things are impossible. The devil would make you believe that an illness is incurable; the idea is to convince you and then you lose out on what God has for you. You must learn how to make the devil flee from you, and that is by talking back to him. There was a preacher who was driving on the highway and he heard the devil mocking him that he had been preaching for many years and had gained nothing from it. The brother packed his vehicle and commanded the devil to get out. Since then, the devil never molested him again. You too can talk back to the devil and he will flee from you. The doctors might have told you that your disease is incurable or that you would need a major operation before you are healed. These are lies of the devil; you should examine what God says about your health. He says that no evil shall befall you. The Bible says that none of the diseases of the Egyptians will come upon you. If you believe God for what He says, then what the doctors say would become lies. The devil has killed so many people with lies like these. When they are supposed to be claiming God's promises, they keep saying that it is a sign of old age.

Sometimes, the devil manufactures problems that make people think that the days of trouble will never come to an end. It is the devil that coaxes people about their beauty and makes them think that they are wanted by every man or woman. He encourages people to alter God's creation in them. He encourages people to be promiscuous, and they think that they are lucky since many men or women want them. Whereas, that is the worst kind of destiny that a person can possibly have. They encourage people to look for evil means of keeping their spouses. The devil would make people listen to his lies and when trouble comes, he would abandon them.

In those days, there was a professor in England, who used to go about preaching in the open market place. He was supposed to be appointed as the Vice Chancellor of his university but the council decided not to appoint him because they felt he would be a disgrace to the university because of his preaching in public. He was not bothered and continued witnessing for Christ. When the council could not find a better qualified person, he was appointed as Vice Chancellor of the university. He did not listen to the lie of the devil, but continued steadfastly in his witnessing for Christ. Today, there are some people who argue against the word of God whereas they have not achieved anything tangible in life. Some scarcely scale through university, yet they argue against the word of God. It is the devil that makes people equate themselves with God.

Immediately somebody realises that the devil is a liar, the chains binding him or her will begin to break and he or she will obtain freedom. It shall be so for you, in the Name of Jesus.

2. The supremacy of God's power over devil's power:
The devil does not want people to understand that the power of God supercedes his own. As far as the Bible is concerned, there are three that bear record in heaven; God the Father, the Son and the Holy Spirit. They form the trinity and are in the third heaven. The second power is the church of Christ on earth. Hebrews 12:23-24 says, *"To the general assembly and church of the firstborn, which are written in heaven and to God the Judge of all, and to the spirits of just men made perfect. And to Jesus the mediator of the new covenant, and to the blood of sprinkling, that speaketh better things than that of Abel."* The next power is God's angels while the lowest power is that of the devil and his demons.

SALIENT FACTS
The devil is not God and cannot be like Him. God did not create the devil; He created Lucifer who fell and turned himself to the devil. The devil is a creature and is subject to the power of God and can only operate with permission; he cannot overpower God. The devil is not above judgement. The church of God is above the archangels, cherubim, seraphim and the innumerable company of angels. Ephesians 2:6 says, *"And hath raised us up together, and made us sit together in*

heavenly places in Christ Jesus." Jesus has been raised to the third heaven, and every other thing is under His feet. If the Church is His body then every other thing is underneath the Church. Jesus says: "The Lord rebuke you satan." The Church would say: "I rebuke you satan, in the name of Jesus." If you have been afraid of the devil, you should stop being afraid. The truth is that, if you know and stay in your position, the devil too will stay in his, which is underneath your feet, not on your shoulder and definitely not on your head.

3. Knowledge of the source of your problem: Many problems would get solved as soon as the source is detected. A problem could emanate from any of the following:

i. Sin: It opens people up to spiritual attacks and kills. It is spiritual leprosy. It is the greatest tragedy that has ever befallen man. God hates sin with perfect hatred. He who commits sin does not know God and is not known of Him. Willful sin is an attempt to overthrow God's kingdom and taking sides with the kingdom of the devil. There is no small sin. Sin has the power to hinder God. That is why the Bible says; "God's hands are not shortened that He cannot save, neither are His ears heavy that He cannot hear, but iniquity has made a separation between God and man, so that He cannot save."

Anyone who knowingly practises sin is lost already. If God could discipline Moses, Ananias and Sapphira and the sons of Aaron who offered strange fire, then it shows that He hates sin. The Bible says, "Though hand join in hand, the sinner will not go unpunished." Whenever there is a problem, make sure you check your life and see if there is any sin there.

ii. Demonic spirits: They cause sleeplessness, horrible dreams, sicknesses, diseases, internal heat, things moving about in the body, hearing strange voices, etc. If you are bothered by demonic powers, I would advise that you go for deliverance.

iii. Self-inflicted problems: It is an amazing fact that many people do things that run contrary to their own peace. They organise battles and vigorously fight against themselves. All the fornication, adultery, abortions, drunkenness, alcohol consumption and smoking that you are committing mean that you are fighting yourself. They make you a candidate in the school of self destruction. The Bible talks about some people who fight against themselves. Anger, malice, impatience etc facilitate self-destruction. Are you fighting against yourself? Repent, before it is too late.

iv. Accidental problems: Some people go to places where they carry the evil load of the enemy. When a person just walks into an environment where there is an epidemic, the person will be affected. There is a Yoruba adage that says, "When a person is asked to help bring down a heavy load, and he lays claim to it, there is a serious problem somewhere." The Bible says that the angels of the Lord encamp round those that fear Him. If your life is dirty, the angels will not be able to tolerate your odour. If your life is chasing away angels, and there are arrows flying about, the arrows will enter into your life.

v. Inherited problems: These are problems that are transferred from parents to offspring. It could be suicidal tendency, broken home, insanity, poverty, persistent problems, etc. They are usually attached to the family roots. As soon as you can trace the history of a problem within a family, you should know that ancestral spirits are at work there.

vi. Curses: These are evil and negative pronouncements against a person. They could result in repeated chronic diseases, marital failure, financial insufficiency, unnatural death, etc.

vii. Spiritual carelessness: Sometimes, the Holy Spirit would be speaking but many people do not listen to Him. Many people are proud and unteacheable. Many are careless in the things that are related to holiness, they take many things for granted and some even under-rate the devil. 1 Peter 5:8 says, *"Be sober, be* vigilant; because your adversary the devil, as a roaring lion, walketh about, seeking whom he may devour."

viii. Evil covenants: An evil covenant is an evil agreement made with an evil spirit. It could be made on behalf of someone. It could be conscious or unconscious. It could be done through rituals or sacrifices, blood bath or drinking, bath at the river or beach, incisions, supply of materials to herbalists or false prophets.

ix. Possession of cursed or abominable things: These are decorations, ornaments, jewelry, and carved wood dedicated to idols. You should know how the Holy Spirit talks to you. Learn how to hear from God, so that you will know what to do at every point in time. A spiritual inventory of your possession is necessary. People criticise the MFM for not allowing people to put on jewelry. It is because we do not want to take chances. Some of the jewelry on sale are items dedicated to idols. Some of them have diabolic inscriptions or images. Some have snakes drawn on them, half moon, eye, some look like a cross but at a closer look, one would see that they are hanks. If we find any door through which the enemy can come in, we block it completely. We tell people the blunt truth, because we do not want their blood to be demanded of us. When the devil sees that his mission to a place is defeated, he tries to water down the efforts of the people there and antagonizes them. I read an article captioned, "The man who refused to die." He was attacked in the dream by a snake; he struggled with the snake but could not get himself freed from it and he shouted: "Jesus" and an angel came to his rescue. The angel hit the snake on the head and it died. The following morning, he got a message from his village that his father was dead and that he had a big cut in the head. He understood that his father was the snake that attacked him the previous night.

An ancient songwriter wrote a hymn, which says: "Jesus has conquered death; death is dead." Many people are toying with the enemy. You have to say: "No, not me!"

4. Sin and sinners are destroyers: Ecclesiastes 9:18 says, *"Wisdom is better than weapons of war: but one sinner destroyeth much good."* The Bible says that sin is the transgression of the law; that is, lawlessness. When God says you should not do something and you do it, it is a sign of lawlessness. No man can break God's law; the person will only succeed in breaking himself or herself. Sin is a sickness that contaminates the whole body. Whenever the enemy wants to get at a person, he manipulates him or her to commit sin knowing that in that state, he or she can neither approach God nor would God answer the person. That is why one of the signs of the end of the age is that iniquity shall abound and the love of many shall wax cold. Sin is like a cloud covering the face of God's blessings. Isaiah 59:1-3 says, *"Behold, the Lord's hand is not shortened, that it cannot save; neither His ear heavy that it cannot hear: but your iniquities have separated between you and your God, and your sins have hid His face from you, that He will not hear. For your hands are defiled with blood, and your fingers with iniquity; your lips have spoken lies, your tongue hath muttered perverseness."*

Sin is a binding rope; it holds man in its power. It is a slave-driver; it embitters the life of the slave. It is a disturber of rest; it causes disorder and anxiety. It is a robber of blessings; it starves the soul. It stabs from the back and overthrows the sinner. During the overthrow, many things will be destroyed. To worsen the case, sin is a keeper of records; it records all sinful acts and recalls them; it leaves its mark upon the path of the sinner. It is a detective; it will turn against the sinner, trail the sinner and find him or her out, no matter how fast the person runs or how cleverly he or she hides.

Numbers 32:23 says, *"But if ye will not do so, behold, ye have sinned against the Lord: and be sure your sin will find you out."* Sin is an accusing witness, it accumulates evidence to the condemnation of the sinner. The Bible then concludes by saying that the person that sins is of the devil. There is no neutral ground. There is no clever sinner. In fact, engaging in any sinful act is foolishness. What a sinner is doing now could affect his or her children, and it might go on for ten generations. Sin has a way of linking itself to other sins and it goes on expanding and gets to the biggest one that eventually leads to death.

Samson was a child of miracle; his birth was prophesied by an angel who gave his mother instructions on how to look after him. God said he was going to deliver his people Israel and he actually did exploits. He carried the whole gate of a city and put it aside. When the problem of Samson was going to start, it started with idleness; he had time to sit in the midst of people and tell stories and give them riddles, then, his eyes began to x-ray women; fornication set in and he began to behold prostitutes. He graduated into disobeying God's instituted law on marriage, which says His children should not be unequally yoked together with unbelievers. Samson asked his parents to marry Delilah for him. What was his reason? She pleased him well. Not because she was a child of God, but because he liked her. Delilah signaled the obituary of Samson. He played with his God-given power and Delilah made him tell her the secret of his power and she sold him out to the enemy. He lost his power and became a grinder of pepper and then died with his enemies. He put the whole nation in trouble; and it all started with 'just a little sin'.

Achan put the whole nation of Israel in trouble by stealing the forbidden thing. Sin destroys body, soul and spirit and causes eternal separation from God. There is no small sin and all sinners are destroyers. Sinners in a fellowship hinder the power of God. They limit the power of the Holy Spirit. It is painful to find that sometimes when the angels of God come into a congregation, they do not minister to some people because such people are not ready to receive from God. There is sin in the camp. Sinners cause dishonour to the name of the Lord and make God look powerless. They block the route of God's communication with them.

Beloved, if you are living in any known sin, you will do yourself and your children, family, the church and the whole world a lot of good by repenting. Do not be the 'Achan' that will bring destruction upon your family because you are destroying yourself and it will affect them. The issue of sin is so serious that God had to send His Son to die for the world, in order to reconcile the world unto Himself. When Adam and Eve sinned in the Garden of Eden, they were chased out of the garden and that alienated man from God. The Bible says: "The wages of sin is death." If you decide to collect 'salary advance' by thinking you are clever, you are playing with fire. Anything you are doing, of which you will be ashamed if people see or hear that you do, is not worth doing. That thing you cannot announce in public that you are doing, because it is not edifying, stop doing it

before you put yourself and other people in trouble.
Depart from it.

5. Everyone is living a borrowed life: Romans 14:7
says, *"For none of us liveth to himself and no man
dieth to himself."* What we do adds to the sorrow or
happiness of other people. Those who love you might
suffer more than you for your evil actions. Many people
think they have the right to do what they like. They live
their life the way it pleases them. Some disregard the
advice of their pastors, counsellors, elders and parents.
Some flout the rules of common sense, so that they can
feel important but such people will soon discover that it
is foolishness. The Bible says that nobody has a right to
live his or her life the way he or she pleases. You and I
are living on borrowed time and we shall account for
every minute and every second. The Bible says we must
appear before the judgement seat of God to give an
account of everything we have done on earth, where
we have been to, what we said or ate, everything'

6. The secret of the power in the Blood of Jesus:
The Blood of Jesus is unique because He was conceived
by the Holy Spirit, and not man. His Blood was not
contaminated; God Himself prepared the body of Jesus.
Jesus is the word of God, so His Blood is of God. Since
blood carries life, the Blood of Jesus carries the eternal
life of God. The Blood of Jesus spells defeat for the
devil and paves the way for us to heaven; it drives

demons out of our way and brings judgement to stubborn sinners. The devil hates people making mention of, or pleading the Blood of Jesus. The Bible tells us that the Blood of Jesus has redeeming power, that is, if a person has sold himself or herself to the devil, he can be bought back by the Blood of Jesus. The Blood of Jesus has forgiving and cleansing power, that is, through the Blood of Jesus, the sins of a person can be forgiven and all filthiness cleansed. The Blood of Jesus has the power to cover and to preserve, so that spiritual contaminators will not enter into a person, place or thing or situation. The Blood of Jesus has justifying and sanctifying power. The Blood of Jesus can speak; if you plead the Blood of Jesus on a situation, since there is life in blood generally, the Blood of Jesus carries the life of Jesus and the Bible says that the Blood of Jesus speaks better things than the blood of Abel, which was crying out unto God for vengeance. The Blood of Jesus has melting, pacifying and confirming power. It is through the Blood of Jesus that we can enter into the Holy of holies, the Throne of God. The Blood of Jesus has life-giving and overcoming power.

John 6:53 says, *"Then Jesus said unto them, Verily, verily, I say unto you, except ye eat the flesh of the Son of man, and drink His blood, ye have no life in you."*

Revelation 12:11 says, *"And they overcame him by the blood of the Lamb and by the word of their testimony; and they loved not their lives unto the death."* The devil hides this information from believers, so that they will not know the power in the Blood of Jesus. A lot of people do not know how to plead or cover themselves with the Blood of Jesus.

7. Healing and divine health is God's will for us: Some people have become so used to sickness, that even when they are not ill, they look sickly. God wants you to be well and healthy; it is the devil that wants people to be sick. If you come to God and there is doubt in your heart regarding His ability to heal you, you might never be healed.

A man of God was ministering at a crusade and spotted a crippled man on a wheel chair, who once in a while, would make some noise with his stump. The minister sent an usher to tell the man not to disturb the audience. When the minister saw that the man kept shaking his body and it appeared as if he was trying to get up from the wheel chair, the man of God himself came close to him and said it was not yet time for him to pray for people to get healed, so he should be patient. The minister discovered that the man could not understand the language that he was speaking and the ushers got someone to interpret. The man said he came to the crusade to get healed and nobody would hinder him, not even the minister of God. When the minister got back to the pulpit, he prayed and said like Elijah: "If I be a man of God, arise and walk!" Before he finished talking, the man got up from the wheel chair and started to walk. The man went there with faith in his heart, with the intention and expectation to be healed, and he got his healing. That is all God is looking for.

Sometimes, people attend prayer meetings because they were asked to come and nothing actually happens. If you go to the presence of God with expectation in your heart, knowing that God is the Creator of heaven and earth, and that the Bible says: "In the beginning, God created..." then, He must have spare parts. If what your health needs is a spare part, He will provide it. If what it needs is servicing, He will bring out all the dirt in you, all the evil food that you ate at the table of the devil and from the hands of night caterers, then, He will drain them out. If it means turning you upside down, He will do it. The Bible says: "He Himself bore our infirmities... and by His stripes we are healed". God has done all the healing; all we need do is to claim and collect it. The will of God for His children is that we be in good health and be free from all sicknesses, pain, diseases and all physical sufferings. God has provided all the necessary weapons to defeat sickness and all the works of the devil.

1 John 3:8 says, *"He that committeth sin is of the devil; for the devil sinneth from the beginning. For this purpose the Son of God was manifested, that He might destroy the works of the devil."* The Bible says that Jesus came to destroy the works of the devil and that He has given us victory over him. Two believers were being harassed at night by demonic forces. They saw scratches on their bodies and were always sick. One of them started to read Psalms but nothing happened and the other discovered what the Bible says about his health, that Jesus had already borne his sicknesses and diseases. He then prayed the prayer of the destroyer; he prayed aggressively declaring that: "Any power that moves close to my habitation to afflict me, receive spiritual leprosy, in the name of Jesus." Those forces never moved close to him again, because he had discovered the right weapon.

God has given us weapons to destroy the works of the devil and has given us abundant life. If you allow the devil, he will come and give you lectures on how the disease that you have kills and will enumerate the number of people that it has killed. When you sit before a television set, he will show you how the disease is killing people day by day. When you pick up newspapers, he will show you statistics about the disease. All these programming is in a bid to get you discouraged and then you give up. Tell the devil that he is a liar, so that he will not tell you more stories.

Disagree with the negative things you have agreed with before. Disagree with the result of the X-Ray or Scan, or the tests that say this or that is positive or negative.

8. The devil is a defeated foe and can be frightened: Colossians 2:13-15 says, *"And you, being dead in your sins and the uncircumcision of your flesh, hath He quickened together with Him, having forgiven you all trespasses; blotting out the handwriting of ordinances that was against us, which was contrary to us, and took it out of the way, nailing it to His cross; and having spoiled principalities and powers, He made a shew of them openly, triumphing over them in it."*

Things that frighten the devil:

a.   Aggressive faith.
b.   Violent prayers.
c.   Holiness.

James 2:19 says, *"Thou believest that there is one God; thou doest well: the devils also believe, and tremble."*

9. The devil has no free gift: This particular point is very important and I would like you to take it seriously because the devil is succeeding through it in the lives of many people. The devil operates a simple primitive 'Trade by barter'. If he gives someone money or children, he will surely take something else in exchange for it. He would either make a person to vomit what he has given to him or her, or allow the thing to kill him or her. Since it is the devil that distributes sicknesses, he has the power to remove them, when he is appeased, but be sure that he will take something back in exchange. He can operate through strange religions and doctrines; he would remove one problem and replace with a wicked, clever and subtle one. Some people will rush to some places because they have leaking pockets. There, they will help them to remove the leaking pockets and replace them with incurable disease. He would remove tuberculosis and replace it with fornication.

Many years ago, there was an article in the papers, where a cemetery guard was asked what the secret of his wealth was; since his normal salary was meagre. He said his 'friends,' the dead, gave him one thing or the other, whenever they went out in the form of living beings. He accumulated such things for years but died a tragic, mysterious death, and all those things disappeared. You cannot collect something from the camp of the enemy and expect God to prosper it. If your money is from the camp of the enemy, you have to do away with it. Some people think they can bribe God; after acquiring wealth from the camp of the enemy, they would sign cheques and distribute money to religious organizations. Some even build prayer houses. They do not know that the devil is still around and will reclaim what they owe him.

If you have taken things from 'sugar daddies' and you still keep them after giving your life to the Lord Jesus Christ, they will serve as open doors to the devil; he will come back. Sometimes, some people pray for the fire of the Holy Ghost to fall on them or the Lord wakes them up in the night to pray. As they start singing in praise and worship to the Lord, the devil can come and remind them of his things that are in their possession. In fact, he will say they have no right to pray because it proves that they are still in his camp. He can even go before God to accuse them and since God is righteous and just, He would see that the devil is correct and turn back with His blessings. This is why, when some people get born again, God drains away whatever they acquired from the world, before He gives them His own. The Bible says, "A man has nothing except it is given him from above." Whatsoever you have and you know that it is not from above, but from the devil, you better spit it out before the devil makes you vomit it in a hard way.

The devil is a hard slave master; he does not tolerate nonsense at all. It is in the house of God that you see people going late to services. It is not done in the camp of the devil, without punishment. It is not possible to go late to a demonic meeting and go scot-free; every offender would pay with the death of his or her first born or another child, or with one organ in his or her body. Many people go to wolves to fight their battles for them. The truth is that there is no prophet that can fight your battles for you. You might wonder why some of them see visions or prophesy and it comes true; it is because you want to be deceived and the devil would bring out some seemingly true things about you, so that you would continue to consult him. By running around prophets, instead of fighting for yourself, you are inviting demonic prophecies. Do not sit tight in a gathering of dead people; saying that it is your family's 'church' or that there is a powerful prophet or prophetess there.

A certain sister was coming to our meetings and her mother did not like it; she said they had a prophetess in their church that could see visions and prophesy. When the sister told me, I asked her to invite the prophetess to our house and she did. When they came in, I asked them to stand as we prayed. The prayer point that I asked everyone of us to pray was: "O Lord, send your fire into my life, in the Name of Jesus." We had not prayed for long, when the 'prophetess' screamed and started to roll on the floor, crying "Fire, Fire" and was wriggling like a snake. The sister then understood the kind of power that the woman had. As they were going back home, the sister asked the 'prophetess' to go home with her and they were fortunate to meet her mother at home. The sister requested that they prayed the same prayer again and the woman demonstrated even worse than she did earlier on. The sister's mother did not need anyone to convince her that she had made a mistake all along. Quite a lot of people have received evil prophecies from evil and fake prophets like that. There are some girls who have become that kind of prophetess because they no longer have sugar daddies who can give them money. They have now turned prophesying into a money-making venture.

10. God has the final say: Proverbs 19:21 says, *"There are many devices in a man's heart; nevertheless the counsel of the Lord, that shall stand."* God is the only One that has the final say on our lives and on things that concern us. Do you feel trapped in any way by a habit, a practice, a nagging thought, a problem, a sickness, and attacks by the enemy? I want you to know that these things do not determine the final say concerning your life. Even if some people are planning to destroy you, whether they are your parents or friends, do you know that they do not have the final say concerning your life? Even if your parents are very demonic and they place a curse upon your life, it is God that has the final say.

The fulfillment of God's word in your life may take some time. Do not be discouraged; He is the God of the suddenly. When God decides to take action on your behalf, your enemies will be caught unawares; they will just find that you are now enjoying life at its fullest. If God decides that you will be president of your country, you become president right from the day He pronounces it. Any other person can contest it but He has already said it concerning you and it shall stand. Since God is the Alpha and Omega, the beginning and the end, it is what He says that matters. Other people might say or do what they like; what matters is what God says about you and your situation. The Bible says we should not accept defeat. Proverbs 24:16 says, *"For a just man falleth seven times, and riseth up again: but the wicked shall fall into mischief."*

Do not bow to the devil or his agents. Do not accept that the devil has the final say. If the Lord has decided that you would have to pass through a specific fiery situation, you have to pass through it. You might have to pass through the waters; through the seas, through the valleys; you have no option; you have to pass through it. In every situation, God has provided a way of escape. Without trial, there is no triumph. When Israel was before the Red Sea and Pharaoh was behind them with his army, God provided a way through the sea. When Goliath was bragging and boasting and threatening Israel, God provided David. When Ahab was troubling Israel, God provided Elijah. Jesus Christ Himself was led by the Spirit into the wilderness and was tempted by the devil and He overcame. Whatever you are going through now is for a while; it will not kill you. Without examination, there is no promotion. God has the final say on your life; not a human being, not a prophet; not a herbalist, not a star-gazer or palmist that has told you that your life will be short. Not even your family record or village idol. God has the power to do whatever He likes and nobody can query Him. Daniel 4:35 says, *"And all the inhabitants of the earth are reputed as nothing: and He doeth according to His will in the army of heaven, and among the inhabitants of the earth: and none can stay His hand, or say unto Him: What doest thou?"*

If you believe that God has the final say concerning your life, I would like you to re-examine these ten things that the devil does not want you to know and then put your knowledge of them into practice and put the devil to shame. The family unit is the nucleus of the society and that is the target of the devil. Once he has a hold on the family set up, he has a hold on the society. That is why you have to barricade your life and that of your family with the fire of the Holy Ghost and with the Blood of Jesus and refuse the devil entry into any aspect of your life. Blessings are supposed to pursue and overtake you; not evil pursuers.

Below are some prayers that I would like you to pray with aggression. Pray them from the depth of your spirit:
1.   I refuse to yield to the commands of the devil, in the name of Jesus.

2.   Stubborn pursuers, be chained, in the name of Jesus.

3.   I break the hold of problematic powers upon my life, in the name of Jesus.

4.   Evil powers in my environment, be roasted, in the name of Jesus.

5.   All evil delegates sent against me, be roasted, in the name of Jesus.

6.   O Lord, speak your words of fire into my spirit, and let them burn away every rubbish in my life, in the name of Jesus.

7.   I refuse to be devalued, in the name of Jesus.

8.   Every evil utterance by satanic agents against my life and marriage, be nullified by the Blood of Jesus.

9.   I challenge my body with the fire of God, in the name of Jesus.

10. Every negative vow that I have made with any man or woman that is affecting me negatively now, break and be cancelled by fire, in the name of Jesus.

11. Every citadel of the enemy in my home, break, in the name of Jesus.

12. I refuse to be a candidate of amputated breakthroughs, in the name of Jesus.

CHAPTER THREE
BLOOD ON THE DOORPOST

Exodus 12:7 says, *"And they shall take of the blood, and strike it on the two side posts and on the upper door post of the houses, wherein they shall eat it."*

Exodus 12:13 says, *"And the blood shall be to you for a token upon the houses where ye are: and when I see the blood, I will pass over you, and the plague shall not be upon you to destroy you, when I smite the land of Egypt."*

There are four instances where God wrought great deliverance in the Bible. The first time was when Joseph saved his people from a great famine by bringing them to Egypt, where there was plenty of food and he was Prime Minister. The second instance is the one in the texts above, where blood was applied on the doorpost and God delivered His people from the great destruction that came upon Egypt. The third one was when David killed Goliath who was bragging and boasting and threatening the Israelites. The fourth was when Samson killed the Philistines with the jaw of an ass. The common thing with these four instances is the shedding of blood.

Psalm 78:49 says, *"He cast upon them the fierceness of his anger, wrath, and indignation, and trouble, by sending evil angels among them."* There are evil angels that can carry out destruction, even at God's command.

Luke 4:18 says, *"The Spirit of the Lord is upon me, because He hath anointed me to preach the gospel to the poor; He hath sent me to heal the brokenhearted, to preach deliverance to the captives, and recovering of sight to the blind, to set at liberty them that are bruised."* Jesus made this wonderful pronouncement about His mission on earth - to deliver.

Obadiah 1:17 says, *"But upon mount Zion shall be deliverance, and there shall be holiness; and the house of Jacob shall possess their possessions."* In order to get delivered, there has to be holiness.

Acts 10:38: *"How God anointed Jesus of Nazareth with the Holy Ghost and with power: who went about doing good, and healing all that were oppressed of the devil; for God was with Him."* Basically, blood on the doorpost refers to deliverance. The devil is an oppressor and Jesus is the One that breaks the yokes of the devil. The battle of life comes upon every man on earth. No one is free from it. Some people come across their own battle very early in life. Jacob started from the womb; he struggled with his brother in the womb and as they were born, his hand was holding on to the heel of his brother. There are many people like that. I know a sister, whose mother used local means of preventing a miscarriage, while the sister was in the womb. A candle was put in a bottle and the bottle was hung somewhere. When the pregnancy was due for delivery, the rope tying the bottle was cut and the baby was born safely. The sister grew up and started to have problems as an adult. Her mother was dead, so there was no one to tell her what was done to her while she was in the womb. It was during deliverance prayers that the Lord revealed the candle in the bottle and it was then that she was able to pray specific prayers.

Many people are battling with the problems that have been in their lives before they were born; yet, they are impatient; they cannot pray for a long time. They want to pray for two minutes and expect a life long problem to just disappear like that. Many people have been members of dead prayer houses for as long as they can remember and their stay there has strengthened their problems. When they come to a place like MFM, they pray for thirty minutes and say that nothing is happening.

Many years ago, I was in a church where we caused a lot of havoc to the kingdom of darkness. Many people gave their lives to Christ and many herbalists lost their clientele. There was a particular one whose third wife came to our crusade and surrendered her life to the Lord Jesus Christ. She decided that she would no longer live with the man as third wife, because she just realised that it was a sin. Soon the herbalist came to us, saying that we should release his wife. We told him that she was the one that did not want to continue living with him. He threatened to fight us with his charms, we told him that it was a good challenge; that he should go ahead. If it was physical fight, we would not be able to lift a hand against him. Since it was his idol, we said he should go ahead. He asked us the kind of power that we had that gave us so much confidence. We told him that it was Jesus. We told him that the Bible says that at the Name of Jesus, every knee should bow, including witches, wizards, herbalists, etc.

There was the case of a woman who consulted a herbalist when she was pregnant and it was agreed that she would pay ₦300 for delivery. On the due date, she went to him and he asked for the money but she did not have money to pay. Neighbours rallied round and were able to gather N150. The herbalist started to chant incantations and the first baby came out; she was expecting twins. All efforts to get the other baby out proved abortive and the herbalist declared that some powers that were stronger than him were blocking the baby. Just then, the woman's husband arrived and he decided to take her to her parents, if she was going to die. She was put in a taxi and on their way, there was traffic jam and someone who knew the woman saw them and asked what was going on and husband said he was taking her to her parents in the outskirts of Lagos. The person asked if they could come with him to his church for prayers and the man accepted. They met the prayer warriors at the church and as soon as they said, "Father, in the Name of Jesus..." the baby just came out hale and hearty. Here were two children born of the same mother, on the same day, but at different locations and different spiritual environments. Many years later, things went really tough for the one that was born in the herbalist's home, until prayer started. Her problems started from the day of her birth.

Another pregnant woman went to the hospital to get delivered of her baby. She could not afford the charges and was retained there. Later, she got a big plastic bag and put her baby in it, and told the nurse that she was going to ease herself. That was how she smuggled her baby out of the hospital without paying the bills. She thought she was smart but she gave the baby a bad foundation. She made the baby to start life as a debtor.

Some people come across their own problems in their youth, some in their old age. There was a couple in court; the man was seeking divorce. He was seventy-five years old and the wife was seventy. She was weeping. The judge was surprised at the man who insisted on putting an end to his forty-five year old marriage. He had a new-found lover that he wanted to marry who was of the same age as his youngest child. This was a deliverance case. There was no blood on the doorpost of that marriage, so the angel of death killed it. Many people do not understand the ministry of deliverance, which is a ministry of conflict and that is why they are suffering, despite the fact that they are born again. They do not understand the fact that there are unseen forces that are militating against the home in these last days and that the only way out is to put the home under the protection of the Blood of Jesus.

Important statements of fact:
1. There is nothing in life that we should fear: We just need to understand the things around us. Fear springs from ignorance. Let it be clear in your spirit that there is nothing to fear. Even if the doctors have written the worst results and have even condemned you to death, there is still no cause for fear. There is a saying that, 'Every man's mountain is his ignorance'.

2. God has decided to save us from defeat, but not from trouble: You cannot be defeated but you have to fight. It is that fight that you are going to do today, as you read this book. The fact is that the home is under attack and there is surely a fight going on. We should not pretend and say 'All is well.' We should face the reality of the fact that there is a problem somewhere but there is a way out because we are the children of the Most High God, the One Who is mighty in battle; Jehovah, the Man of war. Jeremiah 15:20 says, *"And I will make thee unto this people a fenced brasen wall: and they shall fight against thee, but they shall not prevail against thee: for I am with thee to save thee and to deliver thee saith the Lord."*

3. **Most of the time, people underestimate themselves and over-estimate difficulties:** The Bible says, "Forever O Lord, thy word is settled in heaven." It is the word of God that is settled and it stands sure; not your dream, or the prophecy of a prophet. The fact that someone is saying something negative about your situation does not mean that it will be so. Lamentation 3:37 says, *"Who is he that saith, and it cometh to pass, when the Lord commandeth it not?"*

4. **90 per cent of the bad things people think will happen to them never come to pass:** If they are allowed to happen, the devil would give sermons that would make people doubt God and see the negative aspect of things. Most of the time, this leads to discouragement, which makes people lose hope for any improvement. You must understand this very well so that you will take the prayer points in this chapter

seriously, and pray them consistently and fervently until something happens.

5. To draw from your spiritual bank account, you have to deposit something there: The reason many people are being harassed in their dreams is that they do not have much in their account. You have to be prayerful, faithful in paying your tithe and offering and live a life of holiness.

6. God is more interested in making us what He wants us to be than allowing us to become what we would like to be or giving us what we would like to have: That is why God sometimes delays our blessings until we have attained the standard He wants us to.

7. Many people will suffer from the cradle to the grave, unless they go through deliverance: Except some people engage in the ministry of conflict, they will continue to suffer, even though they are born again. I have prayed for someone who vomited a tiny calabash. I have been in a prayer meeting where someone vomited a snake. I have seen a situation where a woman found it difficult to give birth to the baby in her womb. When she was brought to MFM, she was prayed for and immediately, she fell into labour and passed out some pieces of kolanuts, before the baby came out.

The kind of benefit that we derive from prayer is beyond the dream of anybody. The power of prayer is yet to be fully comprehended by mankind. Violence is required to disgrace, chase out, and destroy all those powers that are oppressing our lives. That is why the Bible says, "Right from the time of John the Baptist, the kingdom of God suffereth violence; and the violent taketh it by force."

When the Bible says, 'The violent', it means you have to be fierce and dangerous in action; it means you have to act in great damaging force; it means you have to be unusually forceful. That is why the Bible used that word violence. It means strength, vigour, fervency and zeal. All these put together in the spirit will destroy the powers of darkness. Holy violence is required to do what God wants us to do. We must be involved in contending for the faith. That is why violence is required.

A long time ago, there was a battle scheduled to take place between the Romans and the British. The British Army had mapped out the strategies of attack and defense and was impatient to destroy their enemies. As soon as the Roman soldiers arrived, the British thought their own victory was sure. But to their greatest amazement and utter weakening, they saw the Roman soldiers disembark from their ship and set it on fire. This meant that they were ready to fight and win, without looking back. That brought about the defeat of the British Army. The Bible calls us soldiers; we are regarded as soldiers because we are engaged in a war. We are in a ministry of conflict; as a soldier in God's Army, you are enlisted in a regiment under a Captain, a Commander, whose name is Jesus. A true soldier obeys the captain and shuns other worldly affairs and entanglements. The Bible says, *"No man that warreth entangleth himself with the affairs of this life; that he may please Him Who hath chosen him to be a soldier"* (2 Timothy 2:4).

A true soldier is armed and fit for the work he has been called to do. A true soldier in God's Army puts on the whole armour of God at all times, so that he will be able to withstand the devil. He must put on a uniform to be identified with that Army. The uniform is holiness and the Holy Spirit dwelling in him. A true soldier is known by his habit, armour and weapons. A true soldier has the mandate to discover, fight and destroy his enemies, whether foreign or domestic. A true soldier must be skilled in martial discipline and must know all the portions of war. A true soldier must follow after the leader, must be able to recognise the bugle or alarm, so that when there is a call to fight, he will jump out of his bed and go out and fight, no matter what hour of the day or night it is. A true soldier must be bold and courageous and not be frightened by the threats and strengths of the enemy. A true soldier must endure hardness and prepare himself for it. A true soldier does not befriend the enemy. A true soldier does not turn his back at the enemy, so that he will not be caught unawares.

The kind of battle that Christians are engaged in is a battle that has already been won. Or victory is sure, our weapons are spiritual; our Captain is the best because He is the King of kings and Lord of lords. He has the keys of death and hell. Even if the doctors have condemned you to death, Jesus has the key to your life. Our number might be few, but our side is the stronger one in the battle. The worst the enemy can do will work to our benefit. Take this prayer point: "Every revival of the enemy against my life will work to my benefit, in the name of Jesus."

A man had a disease that the doctors concluded would kill him. He even went abroad but nothing could be done to help him. He was asked to 'put his house in order' and get ready to die. He said he rejected it in the name of Jesus; even though he did not know Jesus then. When he came back to Nigeria, he was brought to MFM and after series of prayers, the Lord restored his health, and he did not die. One year later, he went abroad and decided to pay a visit to the doctor who gave up on him. When that doctor saw him, he fainted. He thought he was seeing a ghost.

People always ask us who needs deliverance. My answer is that everybody needs one form of deliverance or the other; especially Africans, because of our idolatrous background. Many people need deliverance from the spirit of poverty, even though they might have millions of Naira in their possession. It is possible to finish ten million Naira in a day; either wisely or foolishly. The issue of deliverance is often wrongly construed. People always think of witches and wizards when they hear of deliverance. Whereas, a fornicator or an adulterer is a worse deliverance candidate. A person who gets angry is the same as a witch and they both need deliverance. In fact, it is sometimes easier to get a witch delivered, than someone who fornicates or is addicted to smoking or drinking alcohol. There is a spirit behind each of them.

WHEN DO YOU NEED BLOOD ON THE DOORPOST?

- When you find that all your input and effort amount to nothing.
- When you are going backwards instead of moving forward.
- When you suffer unexplainable loss of memory.
- When you always do regrettable things.
- When a rich person suddenly becomes poor or is being continually duped.
- When trials seem to be unending.
- When you are enslaved to sexual immorality.

- When you are sexually confused or perversed-homosexuality, pornography, etc.
- When you feel unnatural movements in your body or head.
- When you are unable to get baptised in the Holy Spirit.
- When you encounter chain problems.
- When you have horrible dreams.
- When you have a sick tongue, that is, you are unable to control your words.
- When you have strange diseases that defy medication.
- When you are involved in idol worship.
- When you have emotional disturbances.
- When you have mental confusion.
- When you suffer restlessness.
- When you hear strange voices.
- When you fear.
- When you experience chains of failure.
- When you are operating under evil covenants and curses.
- When there is evil dedication to idols or spirits.
- When you record failure in your daily Christian living.
- When there is breakdown in marriage.
- When you suffer profitless hard work, fruitless effort, etc.
- When you groan under inherited problems.
- When there is constant harassment by evil spirits.

- When there is evil trend in the family.
- When you suffer failure at the edge of success.
- When there is ungodly soul-tie.

It is easy for these things to hide away under beautiful dresses while they feed fat and fight their victims from underneath. If you have tried everything to succeed but to no avail, you should know that you need deliverance. The first step to getting delivered from any evil is to be born again. Demons tremble when a person surrenders his or her life to the Lord Jesus Christ. It is a spiritual disaster to evil spirits. The presence of the Holy Spirit in the life of a person weakens them and makes it easier to chase them out. The order given them by the devil is to hold people captive at all costs and they do it with fierce determination and resistance because they will face punishment or demotion if they lose their captives. This is why you have to be aggressive in your prayers. Ice-cream prayers will not help at all.

Some people wonder why they still have problems after having gone through several deliverance sessions. It is because complete and true deliverance depends on several things:

1. The condition of the heart. If your heart is filthy and there are strange thoughts going on in it, you cannot get delivered.
2. Faith. Once you believe that your deliverance is settled in heaven, then, it is.

3. How deeply entrenched the evil spirits have been. You do not expect the spirit that has inhabited a life for sixty years to leave at the wave of the hand.

4. Family strongholds that have persisted through generations.

5. Willingness of the person to be free from these evil spirits.

Sometime ago, we were praying for a sister and a voice spoke through her and said we should ask her if she wanted to be delivered or not. We asked her and she said she did not ask us to minister deliverance, that she only asked us to pray for her head to stop aching.

95 per cent of the women in our environment do not enjoy marriage because they are consciously or unconsciously involved in one evil covenant or the other. The demons in this environment have distributed anti-marriage forces into the lives of many women. That is why many husbands are unserious, some die young or are polygamous, and the children are contaminated. These anti-marriage forces cause late marriage and make in-laws to interfere with the lives of couples. Some women get married to old men who treat them like kids and some marry younger men who turn them into boxing partners. Deliverance is needed so that many people will possess their possessions and live a peaceful married life.

A certain man wanted to win in the Olympic Games and so, he went to see a herbalist who asked him for a live snake. He paid the herbalist to get the snake and he did some charms which made him to actually win the gold medal that he wanted. The herbalist programmed the snake to pursue him so that he would run faster than the other athletes. Many years later, after he had resigned from athletics, he felt the snake crawl into his backbone and trouble started. He was introduced to MFM and he went through deliverance. It was then that the snake crawled out of his body.

The virtues of many people have been stolen or buried or hung somewhere. The process for recovering them is deliverance. The process, through which a person can be set free from evil padlocks is deliverance.

How to get complete deliverance:
1. Become born again: Salvation is very important. Changing camps and leaving the devil to go to Jesus would make you free from the shackles of the enemy.
2. Baptism and anointing of the Holy Spirit: When the anointing falls upon you, yokes would be broken.
3. Study and meditate on the word of God: As you read and digest the word of God and renew your mind with it, demonic bondages are broken.
4. Repentance: When an evil spirit is asked to leave and it finds out that there is a little sin in the life of the

person, it will not go. It will actually call for reinforcement from the kingdom of darkness.

A woman had ulcer and went here and there but did not get healed. One day, she met a man of God, who told her that all she needed to do was to stop grumbling and complaining. She did not like the advice and insulted the man of God as she was leaving. When she got home, she did not have peace of mind. She decided to try what the man of God said and discovered that it worked.

HOW OT OBTAIN EFFECTIVE DELIVERANCE

1. **Casting out evil spirits:** This means getting rid of demonic influences, hindrances, sicknesses and eliminating their strongholds.
2. **Violent faith and positive confession:**
   Mark 11:23 says, *"For verily I say unto you, that whosoever shall say unto this mountain: Be thou removed, and be thou cast into the sea; and shall not doubt in his heart, but shall believe that those things which he saith shall come to pass; he shall have whatsoever he saith."*
3. **Maturity in Christ:** As you grow in the Lord, certain things find it impossible to stay in your life.
4. **Spiritual warfare:** The best method of deliverance is praying through by yourself. It is better to learn how to deal with the powers of darkness than to rely on a man of God. It is important because you

might find yourself in a situation where you will have to face the enemy by yourself.

Prayer is very powerful and there is no situation that it cannot change. Prayer has prevailed over fire, water and the earth. It has stopped the sun in its course. Prayer has prevailed over demons. It has prevailed over the devil and cast him down. Prayer has moved angels; when Daniel prayed, the answer to his request was being brought to him, when the prince of Persia waylaid the angel and he could not go. The persistent prayers of Daniel gave the angel victory. Prayers have fetched blessings down from heaven; it has healed the sick, raised the dead, stopped the mouth of lions and put enemies to flight. It has subdued kingdoms, opened prison doors and broken the gates of brass. There is no artillery of hell fire that can stand the artillery of prayers. It is like an engine and it makes the enemies tremble. Woe unto those that prayer powers are targeted against. Woe unto that witch or wizard that prayer powers are targeted against.

I shall not cooperate with my enemies; I hope you will not cooperate with your enemies. I would like you to take the prayers below with the spirit of 'Enough is enough'. Pray like blind Bartimaeus and make sure you get your breakthrough.

However, if you are not yet born again, you might not be able to pray these prayer points effectively. Therefore, I would advise that you first settle your scores with the Lord; see yourself as a sinner and confess your sins to the Lord. Ask Him to forgive your sins and cleanse you from all unrighteousness. Claim the redemptive power in the blood of Jesus that was shed on the cross at Calvary. Invite Him into your life and ask Him to become your personal Lord and Saviour. Enthrone Him over the affairs of your life and submit your totality to Him. Say bye-bye to the world and the devil; make sure you do not go back to them any more.

One day, a certain sister prayed the kind of prayer you find below and got her deliverance. At the age of thirty-seven, she had never menstruated, so she was given this prayer point: "You owners of evil load, carry your evil load, in the name of Jesus." She prayed with holy madness and turned it into a machine-gun prayer. As she was praying with madness, the Lord opened her eyes and she saw an old woman and an angel commanding her to carry her load, which was on the ground. The old woman refused and said she was dead. The angel told her that he did not ask if she was dead or not. She reluctantly carried it and the vision cleared. Immediately, the sister felt blood trickling down her legs. Her menses had started. That is Jesus in action and His power is still available now.

Take these prayer points with all the strength in you:

1. Let my testimonies appear; let my failure disappear, in the name of Jesus.
2. I receive undefeatable victory, in the name of Jesus.
3. O Lord, heal my wounds, in the name of Jesus.
4. Lord, set my broken bones, in the name of Jesus.
5. Every satanic artillery against my life, be roasted, in the name of Jesus.
6. Every witchcraft gathering against my life, scatter by fire, in the name of Jesus.
7. Every destiny demoter in and around my life, fall down and die, in the name of Jesus.
8. Every household strong man, be unseated by the finger of God, in the name of Jesus.
9. Every witchcraft bird flying contrary to my destiny, fall down and die, in the name of Jesus.
10. Every agent of backwardness in my life, release me, in the name of Jesus.
11. Every evil throne installed against me, be overthrown, in the name of Jesus.
12. Every agent of disorder in my life, be scattered, in the name of Jesus.
13. Every power feeding my problems, fall down and die, in the name of Jesus.
14. I release myself from every curse working in my family line, in the name of Jesus.

CHAPTER FOUR
DEEP SECRETS, DEEP DELIVERANCE

Daniel 2:22 says, *"He revealeth the deep and secret things: He knoweth what is in the darkness, and the light dwelleth with Him."*

Some things are deep while others are on the surface. You have to dig deep to get something that is deep. Gold and oil are treasures and cannot be found on the surface of the ground; you have to dig deep to find them. There are some deep secrets about life and the Bible tells us that it is God that knows the secret things and can also reveal them. The word of God goes on to say that God knows the things that are in the dark. One fact about darkness is that the person in it can see the person in the light very clearly but the one in the lighted area would need special anointing to see the person in the dark. Until certain secrets are revealed, it might be difficult to receive some victories. The enemy of our soul fights a very terrible battle for the souls of men. The devil is the father of lies, so his tactics are very deceitful. The devil has no honour or integrity. As far as the devil is concerned, there is nothing like fairness. If you want to destroy your enemy, you would need to know his secrets.

DEEP SECRETS

It is not everyone that calls on the true God: You may be surprised to find that some people pray to petty gods and if you are not careful, you will say Amen to what they are saying. Such utterances that they call prayers are actually incantations. In such utterances, you will never hear the name of Jesus and they will never address the God of Abraham, Isaac and Jacob. They will just say 'god, god'.

1 Corinthians 8:5-6 says, *"For though there be that are called gods, whether in heaven or in earth, (as there be gods many, and lords many.) But to us there is but one God, the Father, of whom are all things, and we in Him; and one Lord Jesus Christ, by whom are all things, and we by Him."*

Many people are being deceived everyday. One day, a certain brother got into serious trouble. He thought he had problems and a friend took him to see someone who could give spiritual assistance. He said when they got there he was taken to a room which was very dark, whereas, it was just 11 am. He also saw birds flying about and was hearing voices, as if the birds were talking. He felt very uncomfortable and got up to leave. Just then, he sighted a Bible on a table and he sat back, reassuring himself that the Bible meant the presence of God. Someone came to 'pray' for him and he noticed that the person was addressing 'the creator' and never mentioned Jesus. He thought he was referring to God the Creator. Before he knew what he had gotten himself into, his three children were deported from abroad in one day. They were not living together but they all met at the airport in Nigeria. None of them brought back anything. They came back empty handed and could not explain why they were deported. That is why we should be careful where we go. If the Holy Spirit begins to rebel within you, it means you are not supposed to be where you are or you are not supposed to be doing what you are doing. If you stay on, you are looking for trouble and are likely to get it.

The devil has an organised kingdom: The devil has followers and emissaries and runs his kingdom contrary to the kingdom of God.

The worst attack comes during sleep: Some of the problems that people are struggling with started at night, during the hours of 12 midnight and 3 am. That is why it is advisable to stay awake and pray during these hours. Matthew 13:25 says, *"But while men slept, his enemy came and sowed tares among the wheat, and went his way."*

If food is taken out of existence, demonic oppression will decrease: A major part of the afflictions of man comes from the food that he eats. It is a serious thing to find oneself eating in the dream. Spirits do not eat food but when they force-feed a person in the dream, the person will experience different types of affliction.

There are some creatures that are used by witchcraft powers to afflict people in their dreams: If you see the following animals in your dream, you should pray seriously because it means you are under witchcraft attacks: goat, cat, rat, bat, termite, serpent or mud-fish.

Agents of darkness like to put on black clothes: Beware of a person who is not mourning but is always putting on black clothes.

People use candles to destroy others: If you have ever been to a gathering where candles are lit to perform rites, you need to go through deliverance.

The enemy can mix with the wind to afflict people: Some people got paralysed or started to have serious ailments after a strange wind blew on them suddenly. I pray that if you have been afflicted that way, you shall be delivered today, in the name of Jesus.

WHEN IS DEEP DELIVERANCE REQUIRED?

When a problem is on the surface, it is easy to get rid of it through prayers within a few minutes or hours. When a problem is deeply rooted, it would require more effort to pull it out. Many people have confessed to witchcraft and one of them in particular was a small girl. She brought a clay pot in which she had seventeen padlocks; it was amazing to discover that she knew the function of each of the padlocks. Out of the seventeen, she had used twelve on her own father. She said she had locked up all the money that the man had, or would ever have in life. If this kind of thing exists, is it not then necessary to take spiritual warfare serious? Imagine a person at a prayer meeting, praying and then three of such padlocks get destroyed and the person is not even aware of their existence, not to talk of their destruction. If such a person is not serious, those three that were destroyed would be replaced by more wicked ones. That is why you have to pray and be sure you pray through.

I would like you to know that there are some problems that are deeply-rooted. There are some problems that people cannot discuss with others, because they sound very strange. For example, there is something called spiritual blockage; people who are experiencing spiritual blockage cannot connect to heaven; there is no vision, no dream, and no prophecy; they see and hear nothing from God. They are spiritually blank, deaf and dumb. Anytime such people decide to fast and pray, it is a serious problem; whenever they pick the Bible to read, they fall asleep, anytime they start to pray, their thoughts wander from one thing to another; they cannot concentrate. Sometimes, when they go through deliverance, they fall sick and land in the hospital. Any method they apply to make progress spiritually lands them in trouble. Such people need deep deliverance.

There is something called dry faith. Somebody with dry faith prays but doubts God in the depth of his or her heart. People who have dry faith cry and weep all the time, despite the fact that they have prayed. They might even prophesy, but they will still cry. Some people have abnormal thoughts; dreadful things are always passing through their minds; strange thoughts about suicide, sex, cruelty, tormenting thoughts etc. For some people, everything would be going on well and they would almost be at the verge of their breakthroughs, when they would have a strange dream and the breakthrough will not come; then there would be a lot of attacks and strange things will happen to them. For some people, there will be no problem when they have no money but as soon as they have money, one thing will pile up after the other, until the money is exhausted. And before money comes again, problems would have piled up, waiting to gulp the money. Such people need deep deliverance.

There is something called prayer-blockage; that is when a person cannot pray on his own. The only time that such people pray is when they are in the church, or in the midst of other people praying. Some people experience excessive tiredness; they are exhausted beyond measure even without doing any hard work. It means the devil is toying with their body. Some people experience inexplicable hatred; people are just hostile towards them without cause; they are not wanted around for any reason. All these people need very deep deliverance.

WAY OUT

Know that there is a problem: Know that something is wrong somewhere. Once you realise the fact that there is a problem, the solution has started.

Pray with desperation: When a person becomes desperate, progress begins. Many people pray but are not yet desperate.

One day, a woman came to me crying, that her husband was always beating her. He would beat her to the extent that she would faint and he would take her to the hospital. I told her that there were two ways to it. She had to pray for the salvation of his soul. The Lord told me that his salvation would come in a hard way and I told her. She agreed to pray those prayer points. The second day of her prayers, her husband was arrested and taken to the police station and later to prison. He had been there for some weeks, when it dawned on him that the beggarly powers that he was depending on could not help him. When the wife paid him a visit the following day, he showed her the incisions on his back and said it was a useless effort. By the time he had spent two months in prison, the wife came to me again, saying that she was tired of going to give him food in the prison everyday. She said she was ashamed of being referred to as the wife of a prisoner. I told her that the Lord had not finished dealing with him but she wanted him out of prison. We prayed and he was released. As soon as he came back home, the beating started again.

When you get desperate, there are some prayers that you will pray. They do not have to be long. There are many Christians who need to pray desperate prayers today. A brother explained his problems and I gave him some prayer points. I told him that the prayers were dangerous because anything could happen. He said he was ready for anything. Within five days of the prayers, the Lord dealt with the 'Troublers of his Israel.

If some people have made a covenant in the dark world, that they would kill a person and the person happens to be a child of God, whatever they do to the person in the dark world would backfire. If the evil doers vowed that they would rather die than see the person alive and prospering, it would come to pass, when the Lord arises on behalf of the person. That is why some evil people that are unrepentant, die when the children of God pray. Some people really need to pray some deep prayers today. There is nothing that prayer cannot do. Prayer can quench fire; it has brought down fire on soldiers and roasted them. Prayer has sealed the mouth of lions.

2 Kings 1:12 says, *"And Elijah answered and said unto them: If I be a man of God, let fire come down from heaven, and consume thee and thy fifty. And the fire of God came down from heaven, and consumed him and his fifty."*

Prayer has pulled down a witchcraft bird from the sky and it became a human being. Prayers have introduced confusion into the camp of the enemies. Prayers have made owners of evil load to carry their evil load. There is nothing that prayers cannot do. In fact, anyone who can really pray has no problem. Many of the churches that did not believe in MFM kind of prayers have started praying now; some are even asking for deliverance sessions to be conducted in their churches.

The prayers below are not for gentle men; they are prayers for mad prophets. When a prophet prays in holy madness, fire falls. Are you tired of the harassments of the devil and his cohorts? Then, you have to become desperate and pray with all the aggression that you can gather. I want you to pray and be expectant. If you pray these prayers fervently and lose your voice in the process, you would have made a good bargain, because you would have obtained your deliverance from those powers that are trying to prove stubborn. These prayers will cause a lot of havoc in the camp of the enemy. These were the kinds of prayers that chased out demons and they were begging Jesus not to send them out.

Beloved, if you have not yet surrendered your life to the Lord Jesus Christ, you cannot really pray these prayers. If you are not born again, you cannot claim to be a child of God and He cannot reveal any secret to you. All you need do is acknowledge the fact that you are a sinner and that you cannot approach God in your sinful state. If you are ready, confess your sins to Him and ask Him to forgive you and cleanse you from all unrighteousness. Claim the redemptive power in the blood of Jesus that was shed on the cross at Calvary for the remission of your sins. Say bye-bye to the world and the devil and make sure you do not go back to them again. Invite the Lord Jesus Christ into your life and ask Him to come in and become your personal Lord and Saviour. Ask Him to take absolute control of your life and all that concerns you. I congratulate you for this decision that you have just taken. It is the most important decision in life; and I pray that it shall be permanent in your life, in the Name of Jesus. I pray that the Lord will write your name in the Book of Life and nothing shall rub it off, in the name of Jesus.

Take these prayers points with holy aggression:

1. Every power circulating my name for destruction, wherever you are, die in, the name of Jesus.

2. Every serpent of my father's house, today is your final day, in the name of Jesus.

3. My destiny, arise from the graveyard and shine, in the name of Jesus.

4. Thou power of affliction, my life is not your candidate, therefore, scatter, in the name of Jesus.

5. Arrow of confusion in my life, backfire, in the name of Jesus.

6. Every owner of the load of oppression in my life, carry your evil load by fire, in the name of Jesus.

7. Blood of Jesus, arise in your power and fight for me today, in the name of Jesus.

8. Every stubborn strongman in charge of my problem, die, in the name of Jesus.

9. Every power that has swallowed my virtues, vomit them and die, in the name of Jesus.

10. Every power assigned to cut my life short and add it to theirs, die, in the name of Jesus.

11. Every power assigned to steal my wealth, die, in the name of Jesus.

12. Every power shedding blood to destroy me, die, in the name of Jesus.

13. O God, arise and do not pass me by, in the name of Jesus.

14. Thou power of the strange children of my father's house, die, in the name of Jesus.

15. Thou power of the strange children of my mother's house, die, in the name of Jesus.

16. Power to be lifted up, fall upon me now, in the name of Jesus.

CHAPTER FIVE
PRAYERS THAT PUT STRANGERS TO FLIGHT

2 Samuel 22:45-46 says, *"Strangers shall submit themselves unto me: as soon as they hear, they shall be obedient unto me. Strangers shall fade away, and they shall be afraid out of their close places."*

Psalm 18:45: *"The strangers shall fade away, and be afraid out of their close places."*

Our fore-fathers in those days were fond of hunting rats. Sometimes, a rat would run into a hole and they would want to fish it out, but their hands would be too short to get into the hole, or would be too big to pass through it. So, they devised a method; they would gather dry grass and prepare a mini fire. The hole would be filled with smoke and the rat would go further into hiding. After some time, when it sees that the smoke is sustained, it would try to run out and the hunters would be waiting at the entrance of the hole with a cutlass, and all alertness to hit it as soon as it jumped out of the hole.

The kind of prayers in this chapter are the kind that would fish out strangers from their hiding places. One big spiritual truth that you would need to learn is that all spiritual things have levels: anointing, prophecy, spiritual sight or vision, spiritual power, prayer, etc. You can change the realm of prayer from one level to another, depending on the situation and subject matter. What kind of prayers have you been praying? There are some prayers that terrify the devil; there are some that do not. Any prayer that you are praying which does not have any impact on the devil, and the enemy is getting stronger, should be examined. Some prayers are mere words which carry no weight in the camp of the enemy at all. Demons can even block some prayers of some people. There are some that they cannot dare to block. Therefore, in matters concerning your home, you need to know the kind of prayers that you should pray.

Gehazi prayed for a child and it had no effect. Samson prayed a prayer and there was no answer. Saul, at a particular stage, prayed and there was no answer. These prayers had no power so, they achieved nothing. Such prayers go up and bounce back, bringing down nothing. God has provided an avenue through which believers can have power backing them up. Acts 1:8 says, *"But ye shall receive power, after that the Holy Ghost is come upon you: and ye shall be witnesses unto me both in Jerusalem, and in all*

Judaea, and in Samaria, and unto the uttermost part of the earth." This is the only outlet that God leaves for us to obtain power. It is the inlet of the Holy Spirit. The Holy Spirit is the power and He enters into everyone who opens the door. His presence within is vital to every activity of the Christian. The trouble with many Christians is that even though they have received the baptism in the Holy Ghost and are filled with the Holy Spirit and He is in them, He is not in control. The Holy Spirit is treated as a guest and not as host therefore, He is hindered in His natural movement. He is tied up and cannot do what He wants to do.

Many Christians are not conscious of the presence and power of the Holy Ghost. Some are partially conscious and can sometimes acknowledge the fact that He is present in a place. If the Holy Spirit walks into a room, in the form of a man dressed in a three-piece suit, many people will not recognise Him. Many are ignorant of the Holy Spirit and some even refuse to acknowledge Him, or to become friendly with Him. This explains the powerlessness of many Christians. When the power of the Holy Spirit is absent in a prayer, it becomes empty words, that are not different from what an unbeliever or a drunkard is saying. That is why we always say that the greatest thing a person can do for himself or for others is to pray. Prayer is an avenue of communication with God. It is also a disinfectant and a preventive means. It can purify an environment and destroy evil

contamination. Prayers do not die. The prayers that some people prayed fifty years ago are working for us today. It means that prayers will out-live those who say them.

Prayer is great power; it is seeking and finding, and a great source of divine inspiration. Prayer changes things. Crying cannot solve any problem. Murmuring, political manoeuvre or manipulation cannot change anything. One great truth that many people do not know is that prayer is a battle and has to do with conflict. We thank God that our own conflict is different from others because our victory has already been decided. Prayer is not the preparation for battle, it is the battle itself. This is why the devil tries to weaken the prayer life of Christians.

Proverbs 24:10 says, *"If thou faint in the day of adversity, thy strength is small."* It is in the day of adversity that your prayers should mount to top gear. The day of adversity is not the day to cry or run away; it is the time to get more aggressive in prayers. Those who do not agree with apostolic praying avoid meetings where aggressive prayers are prayed. I t is not their fault; it is the enemy that wants to destroy them. Prayer is a spiritual force that has to do with spirit beings and forces. A spirit can never be limited by space or material obstruction such as a wall. If you want to go into a room, you will pass through the door, but spirit beings will just appear through the wall, window, roof or ground. That is why you can find demons in a Christian gathering, dispatched to hinder people from being blessed. Also, angels are there to distribute God's blessings. Nothing can obstruct the power of prayers.

I always tell people that they should not allow the enemy to use their legs as chewing-stick or as meat on their rice. God will hold you responsible for whatever you allow the devil to do with your life. Do not be surprised that the witch or wizard that chewed the leg of a believer and sent him to an untimely grave and hell can surrender his or her life to the Lord Jesus Christ. Later, he or she will die and go to heaven. You cannot contest that because the witch of yesterday has repented and surrendered to the Lord Jesus Christ.

Prayer is a serious fight. If you see anyone that does not like praying, the person has an enemy that is greater than all the witches of the world put together. Satan is a great strategist and an obstinate fighter; he will refuse to acknowledge defeat unless he is forced to. The devil will always fight on one's life, as if he was fighting for his own life. When you pray, you are standing on the victory of Jesus. Prayer is standing on one spot and commanding the enemy to retreat and insisting that he leaves your vicinity. The enemy will only yield what he has to leave. Therefore, you must take the grounds step by step. That is why we say that prayer has to be definite. It must be persistent. The enemy will continually renew his attack. Therefore, the ground that you have taken from the enemy must be defended. It is good to get to the Promised Land. When the children of Israel got to the Promised Land, they had to defend their stay there. Prayer is giving God a footing in your life. The more you pray, the more you give God a footing in your life. You cannot adequately define prayer, without adding that prayer is a battle. It is not a play thing that our Saviour had to sweat and agonise in prayer in the Garden of Gethsemane. In the Bible days, people took prayer as serious business. They prayed with different postures; they bowed or knelt or stood. We thank God that He answers prayers.

My appeal to you today is that you take the prayers in this book with holy desperation, pray from the bottom of your spirit. When the devil wants to finish a person, the first thing he does is to weaken the prayer life of the person; and that also applies to a family. There is a saying that the family that prays together, stays together. When the prayer altar of a couple or family is weak, strangers will come in and settle down. A praying family is a formidable force.

Prayer is the only thing that the devil cannot do. He can sing, dance, and even quote Scriptures. There are three groups of angels; the worship angels who just praise and worship the Lord. There are warrior angels, whose duty is to fight and there are messengers who run errands. Gabriel was a messenger angel; Michael was a fighter and Lucifer was a worship angel. That is why we have to be careful about the kind of music that we sing or listen to, if it is not energised by the Holy Spirit, you have to be careful. That is why preachers are skeptical about some musicians who sing to praise men, and then the following morning, they are singing about Jesus. Some believers will buy such records and claim that the person is talking about Jesus. You cannot serve God and mammon at the same time.

The only thing that the devil cannot do is to pray and he would do all within his power to hinder anybody from praying. Prayer is the advantage that we have over the devil. The devil can hinder you from praying by using different methods. It could be through someone that would provoke you to anger and for some days or weeks, you would be unable to pray as you should. When you take a leave off prayers, the devil will seize the opportunity to plant all kinds of silver and iron arrows in your life. When your prayer life becomes weak, you are looking for trouble. If through prayerlessness, you lose any area of your life to the devil, you will lose more if you do not wake up. The holy madness of the early church was demonstrated in their prayer life. They prayed and buildings shook. Some prayed on their knees until those knees could no longer feel anything. Prayer is not 'Just-a-little-talk-with-Jesus-does-it-all.' Miracles are borne in the womb of prayer.

God expects us to be like the early Apostles; so ask yourself if you are fervent in prayer. Are you the persistent type? Are you specific in prayer? Are you the 'Daraprim' type that prays only in church and on Sundays? Is your life shallow and empty as a result of prayerlessness? Prayer entails full concentration. I would like you to note this secret: the oppression in the life of the children of Israel made them to multiply. Persecution brought out the best from the early church. Opposition shows where the real power of God is. The more you spread the fire, the more it burns. Any problem that any Christian might have could be termed as 'Growth classes.' You should see it as an opportunity to become a prayer warrior.

One day, God wanted to do something and Moses asked Him not to do it. God said he should leave Him alone, but Moses refused. It means the prayer of Moses held God's hand from doing what He wanted to do. The Bible says you should not give God peace until He has done what He should do. You must keep bombarding the heavens. This chapter is meant to gear you into prayers that will make every strange thing in your marriage flee out of their hiding places. In fact, they should fade away according to Psalm 18 verse 45.

The whole world can be divided into two groups: the children of the Kingdom and the children of the evil one. There is no middle camp. Anyone who is not sure of where he or she belongs is a child of the evil one. If you are not sure of being with God, it means you are not with God. Anyone who proclaims neutrality is of the evil one because Jesus says: "He who is not for us, is against us." The devil's job is carried out most of the time by those who claim to be children of God. A sheep is supposed to follow the shepherd, while goats jump from place to place. Why then is the goatish spirit entering into the sheep?

When you attend a church where all you do is seeking to be noticed and respected and hailed, you are dead even though you are alive. Why is it that children of God are being pressed down on their beds? Why are they having bad dreams and suffering from one sickness or the other? Why are the children of God dependent on drugs to survive? When you receive the Lord as your personal Saviour, He comes into your life in the measure you allow Him. The life of a Christian is like a big house with many rooms. You have to surrender every room in the house of your life to the Lord Jesus Christ. Any room that you do not surrender to Him will harbour strangers.

Evil Strangers

Evil strangers are hidden spirits. Happy is the man or woman who can yield the totality of his or her life to the Lord Jesus Christ. The devil makes some people poor so that in their search for money, they will come to him and he will deal with them and they will remain his servants. He could make some people rich, so that they will feel they do not need anything and do not have any problem. One truth expressed in the Bible says that godliness with contentment is a great gain. When you envy people and wish you were in the shoes of someone else, or comparing yourself with others, you are not being grateful to God because sometimes, what those people are and have are not to be compared with what God has bestowed upon you and if you are wishing to be in their shoes, you are actually cursing yourself. It could be that the only aspect that is good in their lives is what you are seeing and you are now claiming their kind of life. Such people have strangers hiding in their lives.

Many people are direct tools in the hands of the enemy, because they have refused to surrender the totality of their lives to the Lord Jesus Christ. Some keep their mouths, hands or legs and do not hand them over to God; that is why they can say things that do not edify and do abominable things or go to strange places. Strangers will inhabit such lives. Many churchgoers need to chase out strangers from their lives and homes. Any room in your home that is not yielded to God will be occupied by the devil; if you fence out your sexual life from divine visitation, strangers will occupy it. If it is your attitude to food or communication, the devil will occupy it and attack you from there.

Some people know that they have strangers in their lives but do nothing about it; some do not know. Some people only surrender partially to the Lord; although they sing the song "All to Jesus, I surrender, all to Him I freely give." Afterwards, they 'borrow' their tithe and for three months, they do not pay back. All these things prove the presence of strangers in the lives of people. Some surgical operations would not have been necessary if the spirit behind them had been challenged and dealt with. It is certainly not the will of God for Christians to be cut into pieces. There are some people who have the spirit of unforgiveness, lust, infirmity, etc. Some people claim to have received the baptism in the Holy Ghost and to be sanctified but strangers are still in their lives wrecking havoc. Some people do not want to remain in the state they find themselves but they cannot help it. Others cleverly cover up with the cloak of religion.

It is up to you, to make up your mind to be sincere with yourself and chase out every stranger in your life. When a sickness refuses to go and is resistant to prayers, or one habit is pushing you here and there in spite of all your prayers, it means that there are strangers in your closet. When a person is occasionally sad without reason, or finds it difficult to give towards the work of God, or knows that there are some forces oppressing him but do not know what to do about it, and do not tell the people who can help, the evil forces will continue to oppress him. This is why many people who are supposed to be strong for the Lord are committing sins in secret.

Some sisters in a bid to find solution to their problems have ended up going to bed with so-called prophets. Some were actually raped, while others were made to believe that it was part of the solution to their problems. These sisters were surprised and disappointed but they could not tell anyone. Some of these 'prophets' actually see things. Some are children of God who have backslidden and still have the gift of prophecy, because the gift and calling of God are without repentance. Once He has given them, that is it. If you notice that there is something in your life that is contrary to the will of God and you have fought it without success, you had better seek help, before it becomes a big lion that will eat you up. If you come across a stranger in your life and attack it in faith, treating it as a stranger or an intruder, and you send it out, you would obtain your deliverance. Sometimes, when we ask people to lay their hands on their shoulders and ask the strangers within them to come out and die, they wonder and some even claim that they do not have any stranger in their lives. Some do not realise it until they start a business and the thing collapses. You can issue a decree on a stranger and command it to come out. All the three departments of our lives, the body, soul and spirit can harbour strangers. When you yield your life to the Lord and allow Him to dwell in every aspect of your life, no stranger will be able to dwell in it.

The rich young ruler went to Jesus to ask what he should do in order to gain eternal life. Jesus asked him what the law says and he recited everything. Jesus asked if he had been doing them and he answered in the affirmative. Jesus then told him that he had one more thing to do; he should go and sell his belongings, give the money to the poor and then come and follow Him. The rich young man found it difficult to comply with what the Lord Jesus demanded of him and he went away, sorrowful.

Many people hide the pressure point of their lives. They indicate where God should go and where He should not go. They want to dictate what the preacher should talk about and the area that he should not go. The love of money is a demon; the rich want to accumulate more, so that they can be happy. The poor want to accumulate money because they think that it will solve their problems. Both the rich and the poor are running after the same thing. When you refuse to yield a certain area of your life to the Lord, all sorts of hidden spirits will move in. You must cry to the mountains today and tell them to become fire, so that all the giants that are hiding there will come out running. Let this be clear in your spirit.

When strangers begin to operate in your life and stay there for a long time, they will refurbish the space that you gave to them and make it as comfortable as possible, thereby making it difficult to chase them out. In fact, they will claim ownership of the place because sometimes, their stay there is as old as the person. Those things will stay there unless they are challenged and they will be there until the person dies then, they will jump into another vacant life. They are terrible strangers.

Some evangelists were praying for a lady at a crusade and suddenly, one of them opened his eyes and saw that the lady was just staring at them. She did not close her eyes and was not saying 'Amen'. When they asked why, she said their prayers could not have any effect on her problem. That is the extreme to which the strangers can go. They made the woman to refuse the ministry of prayer. We have to challenge all these things.

One day, a certain brother was praying and he vomited a snake; it was a stranger which the fire of God expelled from its hiding place. Some strangers will respond to some certain things and some will not. There are some prayers that will make strangers to come out of their hiding places and even expel them completely.

HOLY GHOST MISSILES THAT CHASE AWAY STRANGERS

1. Confusion: God released it on those that wanted to build the Tower of Babel. If your husband is flirting with strange women, you can release confusion into their midst and their language will no longer rhyme. They might even have to call you to settle their fight.

2. Pursuing angels: Balaam was hired to curse the people of God and as he was going, an angel was coming to kill him, because he was going to touch the apple of God's eye. It was his ass that saved him. God opened the eyes of the ass to see the angel and He also opened his mouth to speak, since Balaam could not discern that he was treading a dangerous ground. If God could open the eyes of an ass, I am sure He can open your eyes to see heavenly visions. The Psalmist asked the angels of God to pursue his enemies day and night and let them have no rest. When a person is under pursuit, his primary aim would be a means of escape. A thief that is being pursued cannot ask his pursuers to please wait for him to gulp down a bottle of drink. Also, he cannot ask them to wait for him to urinate. That is the condition you must put every stranger that wants to destabilise your home.

3. **Lightning of God:** Psalm 144:6 says, *"Cast forth lightning, and scatter them: shoot out thine arrows, and destroy them."*

4. **Tempest and storms:** Psalm 83:15 says, *"So persecute them with thy tempest, and make them afraid with thy storm."*

5. **Whirlwind of God:** Jeremiah 30:23: *"Behold, the whirlwind of the Lord goeth forth with fury, a continuing whirlwind: it shall fall with pain upon the head of the wicked."*

6. **Disunity:** You can turn the enemies against themselves and command them to start to fight against one another, instead of fighting you.

7. **Blindness:** Elisha used this on the people that were sent to him to arrest him. They did not know him and he asked God to make them blind until he led them away. 2 Kings 6:18: *"And when they came down to him, Elisha prayed unto the Lord, and said: Smite this people, I pray thee, with blindness. And He smote them with blindness according to the word of Elisha."*

8. **Thunder and fire:** Exodus 9:23: *"And Moses stretched forth his rod toward heaven: and the Lord sent thunder and hail, and the fire ran along upon the ground; and the Lord rained hail upon the land of Egypt."* 1 Samuel 7:10: *"And as Samuel was offering up the burnt offering, the Philistines drew*

near to battle against Israel: but the Lord thundered with a great thunder on that day upon the Philistines, and discomfited them; and they were smitten before Israel."

9. Brimstone: Psalm 11:6: *"Upon the wicked he shall rain snares, fire and brimstone, and an horrible tempest: this shall be the portion of their cup."*

10. Terror and noises: 2 Kings 7:5-7: *"And they rose up in the twilight, to go unto the camp of the Syrians: and when they were come to the uttermost part of the camp of Syria, behold, there was no man there. For the Lord had made the host of the Syrians to hear a noise of chariots, and a noise of horses, even the noise of a great host: and they said one to another: Lo, the king of Israel hath hired against us the kings of the Hittites, and the kings of the Egyptians, to come upon us. Wherefore they arose and fled in the twilight, and left their tents, and their horses, and their asses, even the camp as it was, and fled for their life."*

11. **Curse of God:** Pronounce the curse of God on the strangers, as Jesus did to the unprofitable, deceptive tree. Mark 11:13-14: *"And seeing a fig tree afar off having leaves, He came, if haply He might find any thing thereon: and when He came to it, He found nothing but leaves; for the time of figs was not yet. And Jesus answered and said unto it, No man eat fruit of thee hereafter for ever. And His disciples heard it."* Mark 11:21-22: *"And Peter calling to*

remembrance saith unto Him, Master, behold, the fig tree which Thou cursedst is withered away. And Jesus answering saith unto them, Have faith in God."

12. Hedge of thorns: If you pray the hedge of thorns daily around strangers, their friends will begin to avoid them and they will become miserable and hit the rock. Hosea 2:6-7: *"Therefore, behold, I will hedge up thy way with thorns, and make a wall, that she shall not find her paths. And she shall follow after her lovers, but she shall not overtake them; and she shall seek them, but shall not find them: then shall she say, I will go and return to my first husband; for then was it better with me than now."*

I would like you to practicalise the use of these Holy Ghost missiles. You must make sure that they produce results. I want to encourage you to pray them seriously and not allow your heart to wander. First, ask God to forgive you any sin that could make the strangers to sit tight in your family and hinder the answers to your prayers.

1. All unprofitable strangers, I command you to flee from my life, in the name of Jesus.
2. I challenge every stranger in my life with the thunder and fire of God, in the name of Jesus.
3. Father Lord, You are the Great heavenly Surgeon; perform an operation in every area of my life and where necessary in my family, in the name of Jesus.

4. Everything that has been destroyed by strangers in my life and family, be restored, in the name of Jesus.
5. O God; arise and scatter every power planting unprofitable seeds in my life, in the name of Jesus.
6. Planters of evil seeds, I uproot your evil plantations from my family, in the name of Jesus.
7. I fire the bullets of the Holy Ghost upon every evil spiritual follower in my home, in the name of Jesus.

CHAPTER SIX
SAFEGUARDING YOUR HOME

A certain sister was jilted and she almost killed herself. Everything had been put in place for the wedding only for the man to say that he was no longer interested. Someone saw the way she was behaving and brought her to MFM. She was given prayer points to pray and she did. I asked her about her family and she said there were three sisters and three brothers; none of them had a settled home; including the men. One thing or the other would happen and they would pack it up. Some of them had never even attempted marriage before. I told her that it was a curse which must be broken. I asked if they were Christians and she said they were. I asked her to invite them to the church for family deliverance. They came and prayers started for several weeks. The Lord delivered them and one after the other, they all got married that same year. That shows what God can do in a single operation.

Some women think their husbands are very difficult and that nothing can change them, they do not know the power of God. They do not know that an encounter with the Lord will change every thing. Some years ago, the

Lord told me that three husbands that had walked out on their wives would come back home. A few days later, the Lord did it. One of the sisters said that her husband left eleven years earlier and had even been living with another woman but he came back home. That is what the power of God can do in a single operation.

Many sisters do not have faith. Most of them are like the traders who are selling their wares on the streets and occupying illegal grounds, where officials of the Town Council can come at any time and chase them away. Sometimes, it is policemen that come. In such situations, sales cannot be stable and sometimes, they lose some of their wares, in a bid to run away from the officials that are chasing them. When asked how they are faring, they would say that it is God that gives profit; this is because the Town Council officials have not come to harass them. Sometimes, when sales are bad, they will say they do not know this kind of God that does not give them profit. Many sisters give up at the edge of their breakthroughs and come up with the excuse that there is a limit to human endurance.

A certain woman was separated from her husband for many years. One day, during a service, there was a word of knowledge, that there was a woman in the congregation whose husband left many years ago, that if she could go on a three-day prayer and fasting programme, the Lord would restore her marriage. The woman claimed it and took up the challenge. She fasted and prayed for three days. After service one Wednesday evening, as the she was leaving the church, she heard a voice behind her saying: "So, you too come here!" And the person grabbed her hand. She looked back and behold, it was her husband. She was too shocked to believe what she saw. I am happy to tell you that that marriage has been restored. It tells you what God can do in a single operation.

God will not tell you when and how He is going to do something; but when He has decided to do something, nobody, no power can stop Him; not even you, the person concerned. However, if you get discouraged or renounce God at the moment you are supposed to cling to Him, you will lose out on what He has in store for you.

Ecclesiastes 9:10: says, *"Whatsoever thy hand findeth to do, do it with thy might; for there is no work, nor device, nor knowledge, nor wisdom, in the grave, whither thou goest."* If it is prayer that you have been asked to pray concerning your problems, pray with all your might. If it is fasting that you have been asked to do, do it with all your might and then wait for God to do His own part.

A certain woman was leaving in the same house with her husband but her bedroom was on the ground floor of the duplex, while her husband's own was upstairs. Her husband's mother too was leaving in the same house and her bedroom was upstairs, close to the man's own. Once in a while, her husband would pass the night in her bedroom and whenever she attempted spending the night in his own room, the mother-in-law would object to it. Even if she tip-toed to her husband's door, the mother-in-law would know and would come out of her own room and chase her back downstairs. This woman got fed up. Someone introduced her to MFM and she started to pray. One day, she attended a prayer meeting, where we discussed the message entitled, "Tower of Babel." After the message, we prayed a particular prayer point which says: "O Lord, confuse the language of all evil associations gathered against me, in the name of Jesus." The sister prayed the prayer point fervently. When she got home, she saw that there was a quarrel and her husband had asked his mother to leave her room upstairs, and move into the guest-room downstairs where she was occupying. He then asked his wife to take her rightful position in the home. That is what the power of God can do.

Another woman was living in England with her husband. But since she got married, things were not going on well with her. Things were so bad that she had only two dresses. As cold as the country was, they could not afford any form of heater. Things were really bad. Her husband had no job and she was planning to leave him. The Lord ministered to her that she should not leave him. Later, the man got a job as a waiter a restaurant where he was earning a few pounds. One day, as he was going about his duty, an Arabian came to the restaurant. He had ordered for different kinds of food but found that he did not like them. The Arab started to lament, that he had wasted money because he could not eat what he had ordered. He was talking aloud in Arabic and was wondering how he would survive in that place without understanding or speaking English. This waiter heard him and understood what he said and moved close to him to ask what he could do to help him out of his predicament. The Arabian was so excited to hear someone speak his language that he said he would employ him immediately as interpreter. The waiter asked him how he expected him to leave his regular job for a one-month casual as interpreter and guide. The Arabian offered him an amount that his regular job could not fetch him in ten years. He accepted the offer and that was how his situation changed in just one day. This one-month job broke the staff of poverty in that family and the woman did not leave. In one single operation, there is nothing that God cannot do.

I started this chapter with these testimonies because of what I know that the Lord is going to do in your life, through your reading this book. They are meant to give you an idea of what the Lord intends to do in your life, especially if you have faith.

PERTINENT QUESTIONS

1. Why do homes break?: The devil hates a peaceful, stable home and he is aware of the fact that if he is able to destroy the home, he will destroy the family and then he will be able to destroy the society, then the town and then the country. Everything starts from the home; good or bad. It is a very important institution. Every united home is a threat to the devil; so he tries to pull down the home. Most of the time, when people are trying to settle a quarrel or a fight between husband and wife, they do not seem to see the devil behind their actions and words. If God should open your eyes, you would see that it is the devil that issues the evil commands that make a husband to give his wife a slap. He would go to the wife too and say she should bite the husband and then cry out in a scandalous way to attract the attention of neighbours. It is the same devil that would make the man decide to go out and get a girl-friend who would respect him and he would start keeping late nights or even sleep out. The same devil would tell the woman that she has lost her husband to a strange woman and then give her hypertension.

Malachi 2:16 says, *"For the Lord, the God of Israel, saith that He hateth putting away: for one covereth* violence with his garment, saith the Lord of hosts: therefore take heed to your spirit that ye deal not treacherously." God hates divorce or even separation. Jesus came to heal broken hearts and broken relationships. 1 Corinthians 7:27: *"Art thou bound unto a wife? Seek not to be loosed. Art thou loosed from a wife? Seek not a wife."*

2. **What do you do if you notice that your home is not what you want it to be?:** What do you do when your home is broken but still looks as if it is still together? Today, we have a lot of marriages of convenience. In such cases, things are not getting on well, but the spouses are still living in the same house, because they cannot announce their willingness to separate. They are patching things up. Sometimes, the ladies involved would have been warned by their parents or friends against going into the union but they insisted that that was what they wanted. So, when things go wrong, it would be difficult for them to say it out. They will not be able to go back to their parents and cry out for help or leave. It is a very frustrating situation.

What to do
1. **Find out the cause of the problem and be honest with yourself:** Many people do not consider the role they play in a relationship or its attendant problems. They are quick to point accusing fingers at the other party. If people would be sincere and point accusing

fingers at themselves first, a lot of problems will be solved. There are some things that people should take note of. For example, the fact that nobody is perfect. Occasionally, the imperfection in your partner will show up. What you should do is to recognise the fact that he or she is a human being, and has some weaknesses. Take the person as he or she is, or help him or her to get out of the weakness. Do not feed it by pointing it out all the time or accusing the person every time. If you keep feeding the weakness of you spouse, the wound will get bigger every day. Some women do not know how to cook. If that is your problem, and the object of complaint from your husband, you have to learn how to cook. If the bone of contention is uncleanness, change! Some people cage themselves. They withdraw from everyone and stay apart and even refuse to talk to their spouse. When they get out of it, they smile again. The source of such things should be discovered. The fact is that a strange woman should not be able to overthrow a believer from her matrimonial home, if she is on fire. Who is a strange woman, where the angels of God are?

2. Reject the spirit of divorce: There is a spirit attached to divorce and it is a very terrible spirit. It is a quiet spirit. If it moves in and you do not locate it in time and chase it out, it will cause trouble.

3. Forgive each other: It could be difficult but it has to be done. There are men who just get up and say a prophet told them that their wives are witches. Some of these men, without thinking twice, come home and ask their wives to leave. One would wonder if the women just became witches, or had been and they have stayed that long together and have had children and have built a house together or carried out other projects together and they have been successful so far. When God starts the judgement of these so-called prophets, it will be terrible because they have caused a lot of problems in the lives of many people. They have caused so much trouble and heart attack and broken homes. They call people's friends their enemies and their enemies, friends. The person they are dealing with would not know that they are trying to finish him up. The aim of the enemy is to take away the woman that has been serving as spiritual covering to him, so that they can deal with him. If you do not understand that it is a spiritual battle, you will make an issue out of nothing.

4. Forgive every strange man or woman involved in your marriage: Some women physically fight strange women that are going out with their husbands. They forget that the Bible says that the weapons of our warfare are not carnal; but are mighty through God to the pulling down of the strongholds of the devil. Your weapon is not boxing and fighting and verbal abuse, but has power in God to pull down strongholds. The Bible says, "If your enemy is hungry, give him food; if he is thirsty, give him water." If the Bible can say this of your enemy, it means you should be able to do more to the strange woman. The Bible says by so doing, you are heaping coals of fire on the head of the enemy. Therefore, if there is hatred in your heart for any strange woman, you should get rid of it and forgive her. That is, if you want God to intervene. If you do not forgive, the devil will quote this same Scripture before God and give reasons why your prayers should not be answered. God is just. When the devil reports a person to God, He will see the truth in his allegations and will have to treat the person accordingly. You cannot tell lies before God; so, the devil speaks the truth when he is reporting people. The Bible calls him 'the accuser of the brethren'

5.   **Learn how to release your husband from the bondage of sin:** 2 Corinthians 10:3-5 says, *"For though we walk in the flesh, we do not war after the flesh: (For the weapons of our warfare are not carnal, but mighty through God to the pulling down of strong holds;) casting down imaginations, and every high thing that exalteth itself against the knowledge of God, and bringing into captivity every thought to the obedience of Christ."* You should understand that there is a spirit attached to sin and if a person is not in the Lord or is not led by the Spirit of God, sin will

surely have dominion over the person. You can help your husband by doing the following:

a. **Pull down every anti-marriage stronghold in his life:** Many men have been caged by forces that do not want their lives to have a headway. If a woman gets her leg broken in an accident and her husband leaves her because her legs are no longer straight, you should know that there is something behind it. Some are in seven different cages and do not know it. Their freedom could require seven days fasting and prayers. If a person who is concerned finds it difficult to fast till 12noon, he needs help. If you are his wife and you are nagging, instead of helping him out, you are creating more problems for him. It might be difficult for him to get out of the bondage and at the end of the day, God will blame you for strengthening the bondage of your husband. Many women strengthen the bondage of their husbands by reporting them to all and sundry; they call them all sorts of names and tell the children that they are useless. This idea will sink into the heads of the children and they will start to see them as such.

b. **Bind the strongman in charge of his life:** Mark 3:27 says, *"No man can enter into a strong man's house, and spoil his goods, except he will first bind the strong man; and then he will spoil his house."* It might take you a whole night to pray through, it might take more, depending on the strength of that strongman. This means that you can pray one prayer point for three days, before the person can experience any freedom. Sometimes, when you pray even for three days, the man would come back home drunk, with lipstick patches here and there. You would wonder why the man did that again after praying and fasting for him for three days. It is because the devil wants to discourage you and wants you to give up on him. That would cancel the three-day operation; unless you start all over again. If you understand spiritual warfare, you would know that it was meant to discourage you and you just laugh over it.

If you want to break a wooden bench, you would have to deal heavy blows on it before it would break. The time it takes it to break depends on your own strength and on the thickness of the wood. Some people might deal three heavy blows on it and it would break. Some would have to try twenty blows. A weight lifter might just deal a blow on it and it would break. The fact that a sister fasted and prayed for three days and her home was restored does not mean you will pray for only three days. You might have to do just one day, or up to one month to get your own home restored. It depends on your spiritual strength and the strength of the problem that you are facing, and the strongman in charge of the case. If there is a strongman in a family, and his duty is to see to it that all the men in that family do not get married and settle down with any woman, you have a battle to face. It is a problem that is like an umbrella. It is shielding every member of the family so, you have to find a way of shifting it off your husband's head, or remove him from its shade. However, if the whole family agrees, every member can be set free by getting the umbrella burnt to ashes.

c. **Build a hedge of thorns around him:** Hosea 2:6-7 says, *"Therefore, behold, I will hedge up thy way with thorns, and make a wall, that she shall not find her paths. And she shall follow after her lovers, but she shall not overtake them; and she shall seek them, but shall not find them: then shall she say, I will go and return to my first husband; for then was it better with me than now."*

This is a very difficult prayer point for some women to pray; but it is effective. We usually do not recommend this prayer point, until we are sure that the person is really ready to pray through. If you build a hedge of thorns around a person, it means the person cannot move about without being pricked by the thorns. This is the prayer point that the woman I mentioned earlier on, prayed and her husband landed in prison. He was coming round to his senses and got his charms burnt, but the wife gave up just before he surrendered his life to Christ. He was released from prison but he continued to beat her. When you pray a hedge of thorns around a person, you have to be ready to stubbornly pray until something good happens. If you are too merciful and do not want the thorns to tear the skin of your husband, then, you should not pray this prayer. When you want to go into this kind of prayer session, you would have to confess some Scriptural verses.

SCRIPTURAL CONFESSIONS FOR SAFE-GUARDING THE HOME

Romans 5:5: *"And hope maketh not ashamed; because the love of God is shed abroad in our hearts by the Holy Ghost which is given unto us."*

Philippians 1:9: *"And this I pray, that your love may abound yet more and more in knowledge and in all judgment."*

Colossians 3:14: *"And above all these things put on charity, which is the bond of perfectness."*

Colossians 1:10: *"That ye might walk worthy of the Lord unto all pleasing, being fruitful in every good work, and increasing in the knowledge of God."*

Philippians 2:2: *"Fulfill ye my joy, that ye be likeminded, having the same love, being of one accord, of one mind."*

Philippians 2:13: *"For it is God which worketh in you both to will and to do of His good pleasure."*

Philippians 4:17: *"Not because I desire a gift: but I desire fruit that may abound to your account."*

Ephesians 4:32: *"And be ye kind one to another, tenderhearted, forgiving one another, even as God for Christ's sake hath forgiven you."*

Isaiah 31:7: *"For in that day every man shall cast away his idols of silver and his idols of gold, which your own hands have made unto you for a sin."*

1 Peter 3:7: *"Likewise, ye husbands, dwell with them according to knowledge, giving honour unto the wife, as unto the weaker vessel, and as being heirs together of the grace of life; that your prayers be not hindered."*

Ephesians 3:17-18: *"That Christ may dwell in your hearts by faith; that ye, being rooted and grounded in love, may be able to comprehend with all saints what is the breadth, and length, and depth, and height."*

Jeremiah 1:12: *"Then said the Lord unto me, Thou hast well seen: for I will hasten my word to perform it."*

1 Corinthians 7:14: *"For the unbelieving husband is sanctified by the wife, and the unbelieving wife is sanctified by the husband: else were your children unclean; but now are they holy."*

Job 22:28: *"Thou shalt also decree a thing, and it shall be established unto thee: and the light shall shine upon thy ways."*

Psalm 32:8: *"I will instruct thee and teach thee in the way which thou shalt go: I will guide thee with mine eye."*

Psalm 24:1-2: *"The earth is the Lord's, and the fullness thereof; the world, and they that dwell therein. For he hath founded it upon the seas, and established it upon the floods."*

THINGS THAT WEAKEN THE HOME

1. Expecting your spouse to know what you need without telling him: Your backgrounds differ likewise your needs. You should not assume that your husband or wife knows what you are going through, without saying it out.

2. Independence: When you make your spouse feel you can stand on your own, you are indirectly saying that he or she is useless. It creates a wall and could make him or her find solace outside the home.

3. External consultations and interference: Do not allow a third party between you and your spouse, no matter how close you are to the person. A so-called close friend or relative could be an agent of destruction. Examine the spiritual state of your friends before getting close. No matter how close you are to anyone, he or she should not come between you and your spouse.

4. Lack of mutual respect: Spouses should place a value on each other and on themselves, so that they will have respect for themselves and the ideas of one another. In the African setting, people do not call their elders by name. Once a person is up to a year older than you are, he or she is considered as an elder. It is assumed that a husband is older than his wife. Even if they are of the same age, a husband is the leader of the family and the Bible says he is the head of the wife. It is therefore expected that the wife should give the husband the leadership role, even if she is older or richer or more popular. Some women call their husbands by their names, as everybody calls him. We encourage wives to give their husbands a unique name that would show that they love and respect them; a name that is between them only.

Some women find it difficult to genuflect as they greet their husbands. When they even offend them and they are advised to go on their knees to apologise to them, they find it difficult to do; whereas, they do it to other people outside. When you go on your knees to apologise to your husband, it will not be written on your forehead; even if it is, he is your husband anyway. This is very important, especially in the African setting and if you are an African. There is no home without trouble. Everybody should learn how to keep peace within. Sometimes, you might have to apologise even when you are right. You would be obliged to do some things for the sake of your children, on whom you will give an account to God. Luke 11:17: *"But He, knowing their thoughts, said unto them, Every kingdom divided against itself is brought to desolation; and a house divided against a house falleth."* Unity is very important in the home. When you are united, no enemy or unfriendly friend can penetrate.

5. Taking decisions without mutual agreement: When you take laws into your hands without consulting your spouse, you are inviting trouble, because it means you are not taking him or her into consideration. However, there are occasions where you might have to use your discretion and act on behalf of both of you.

6. Wanting to have your own way: Some women have their way by nagging; some by weeping. Some men have their way by threats or actual beating. Quarrels bring cracks in the wall of marriage or the home..

7. Neglect of body, hair, general appearance and the home: Some women take their looks for granted, when they get married. This serves as excuse for the man who is prone to having girl friends. They would prefer to go out with the single lady who has a flat that is clean and is ready to look after them and be at their every beck and call. Some of these men get disappointed when they find that the girlfriends cannot keep anything clean by themselves. They get it done by other people only to impress them. The hair on the head of a woman symbolises that she is under authority. Sometimes, the hair of a woman tells you much about her. The hair-style of some women is more masculine than feminine. You can recognise the women that are frustrated from the state of their hair. You will know if they are proud or not, whether they are soft or not, patient or not disciplined, organised or disorganised. One day, I saw a colleague of mine who had a strange hairstyle that was very elaborate and it actually looked like a pyramid. I felt sorry for the patients who went to her for treatment.

There are some little things that should be put into consideration, especially if your husband is not born again. Some men are attracted to other women, because they have or do some things that their wives at home cannot do or neglect. A woman, who eats without measure grows fat and easily gets exhausted and would be panting after walking a short distance or climbing the stairs. That could put her husband off and make him to love her less.

8. Impatience: Patience is the greatest virtue that God has given to man. A Yoruba adage says, "Patience can cook a stone until it becomes soft."

9. Intolerance: A couple should be able to tolerate each other's weaknesses or shortcomings. There are some things that can be changed, but there are some things that one has to take the way they are in the life of the other person. Snoring is not interesting; in fact, it could be very disturbing but if your husband snores and you cannot help him find a solution to it, you have to tolerate it. You are not supposed to have a separate room because your spouse snores.

10. Failure to forgive: The Bible says you should not allow the sun to go down on your anger. Do not go to sleep without settling your quarrels or misunderstanding. It opens the door to the enemy to come in.

11. Comparing your spouse with other people: Your husband or wife is unique and should be treated as such. What is good for Mr. A. is not necessarily good for Mr. B. or Mrs. C.

12. Lack of submission: Ephesians 5:22-24 says, *"Wives, submit yourselves unto your own husbands, as unto the Lord. For the husband is the head of the wife, even as Christ is the head of the church: and he is the Saviour of the body. Therefore as the church is subject unto Christ, so let the wives be to their own husbands in every thing."* Ephesians 5:33: *"Nevertheless let every one of you in particular so love his wife even as himself; and the wife see that she reverence her husband."*

The principle is very simple. If you want to catch a monkey, you have to behave as a monkey. If you enter into a colony of monkeys, all the monkeys will run away or even attack you. If you go in on all fours, they will gaze at you and say to themselves, "This is a bigger monkey" and in curiosity, they will move close to you and you will be able to catch them. This means you have to give room to the opinion of your spouse. If a husband loves his wife, he would listen to her advice, and not impose his own ideas on her. The wife too should not insist that her own idea is the right one. Sometimes, even though you are very sure that what you are saying is the right thing, you would have to let go for peace to reign. That way, you will win your spouse over to you. That is what some women do and they are said to have charmed their husbands. Argument leads to quarrels. Sometimes the male ego wants to impose itself. What a wife should do at that time is to do what her husband wants rather than argue with him and give reasons why the idea will not work. I am not referring to sinful acts. If your husband says you should carry or take hard drugs or kill, you have to refuse vehemently and the Lord will back you up.

It might take you one or two years to win the confidence of your spouse. While waiting, you have to let your own ego die, especially the woman. She should do things the way her husband wants them done. Since she dropped her surname to take up her husband's own, she has become one with him and what the Lord demands of her is total submission. By the time your husband finds that your advice is not meant to lord it over him but help, he will not take any decision without first consulting you. If you start proving to him that you are not a fool, that you are learned and that you have one degree or the other, that is pride and you are looking for trouble because you did not marry your degree; you are married to him and the Bible says he is your head. However, the husband too should love his wife as the Lord Jesus Christ loves the church and gave Himself for her. Argument is one of the first things that leaves a crack in the wall of the home. Even if what your husband wants you to do looks absolutely foolish, do it without arguing. When that fails, he will do it your own way.

Food for thought:
"Argument is a display of ignorance, while discussion is a display of knowledge." All these things that weaken the home are meant to give way to the enemy from outside to overthrow it.

Mark 3:24: *"And if a kingdom be divided against itself, that kingdom cannot stand."* Marriage is an institution ordained by God Himself. It is between two people, who have become one. The Bible says that two are better than one. One shall chase a thousand, but two shall chase ten thousand. Jesus, while sending His disciples out to preach, sent them out in twos. When two people are in agreement, they work better.
Amos 3:3 says, *"Can two walk together, except they be agreed?"* The answer is 'No'.

The different stages in a marriage:

a. Honey moon stage: It is the chameleon stage, where each of the spouses hides what he or she really is.

b. Normal stage: This is the time when the eyes of both of them open and they see each other the way they really are. That is when the woman will know that her husband snores, does not change or wash his underwear. At this stage, if you allow the Holy Spirit to take charge, things will balance up. If not, it will get to the negative stage.

c. Negative stage: Here, there is usually a lot of nagging, and noting of petty things that should be neglected. One person may see the other as spending too much time at work and neglecting the home, etc. That is when a woman would notice that her husband does not tell her that he loves her. It is good to say: "I love you" to your wife and it should come from the heart. Those words should not be empty words. The negative stage should not be allowed to get to the excessive stage.

d. Excessive stage: This is when a couple starts hitting each other. It is at this stage that they could start going from one prophet to the other, seeking solution and most times, they get into more trouble through the ritual that those fake prophets or herbalists will perform. There was a woman that poured water on her husband while he was sleeping and the husband too got up and broke the television set on her.

e. Avoidance stage: This is when a couple starts to avoid each other. This is sometimes due to the stories that they have been told by the herbalists or prophets. This could lead to divorce and sometimes, death.

There is no home where there will be no rain or sunshine. Apart from the things mentioned above, that weaken the home, there are some external factors which militate against the home and that is actually the subject matter of this book. We must to know how to guard the home against the intruders.

In Africa, many things militate against the home. Part of what we are meant to do through this book, is to deal with these things. You would have noticed that the black woman has a raw deal on marriage. She is the one that suffers most of the time, if anything should go wrong with the home. In Europe or America, a man would think twice before suing for divorce, because he might end up being homeless and without money. Everything would have gone in favour of the woman.

ENVIRONMENTAL FACTORS THAT MILITATE AGAINST THE HOME
1. Competition from strange women/girls: Man could be said to be polygamous in nature, except he has been regenerated by the blood of Jesus. The unregenerated man a tendency to flirt with other women. One thing is certain: there is no strange woman who would not want

to be the wife in the home. It gets to a stage where the strange woman would want to overthrow the legally married wife of a man because she wants to have him to herself. She is ready to go to any length to get him and that could mean killing the real wife.

One day, one woman was in her sitting room when another woman suddenly came in and congratulated her for taking good care of her husband. She then said she would like to borrow him from her for two weeks. To the utter amazement of the woman, her husband went into the bedroom and came out with a travelling bag. He went away with the woman for two weeks. Obviously, that was not an ordinary woman. She could not have had that kind of boldness, without the backing of some strange powers. If you are reading this book and your husband has fallen into the hands of such women, the chain binding him will be broken today, in the Name of Jesus.

2. Demonic in-laws: When the parents of either of the spouses are demonic, there is trouble. Some parents do not want their children to get married under the pretext that they will not look after them if they get married. If such sons or daughters happen to get married by any means, these parents will not allow them to rest; they will keep attacking their spouses. This is not common in other continents of the world.

3. Financial failure or poverty: As soon as some people get married, their finances go down the drain. They now start struggling to make ends meet. Sometimes, couples accuse one another of being the cause of their predicament.

4. Spirit husband or spirit wife: If a woman keeps having sex in the dream, she should go for deliverance. Usually, spirit husband or spirit wife makes it almost impossible for people to get married, but when they do, the spirit husband or spirit wife keeps attacking their spouses. In the case of the man, the spirit husband of his wife could make him poor or even kill him at a young age. And in the case of the woman, the spirit wife of the man would keep molesting the wife; and could hinder her from getting pregnant, or make her to continue having miscarriages and could kill her. Spirit husband or spirit wives make the physical sexual life of a couple unbearable, unsatisfying and disgusting thereby making one or both of them disinterested in mating. They could eventually get the home broken. It is after the couple would have separated and gone their different ways that they realise that it was not normal for them to have separated. Sometimes, it is too late, because one could have started a new life with someone else.

5. Demonic mark: This makes it difficult for people to get someone to marry. Sometimes, victims go from man to man or from woman to woman, who are not ready to marry them. If they are allowed to get married, their spouses could die. If they remarry, the new ones too could die.

6. Anti-marriage spirit: This spirit does not want people to get married; if they eventually do, it will cause a separation. That is what makes people lack respect for their spouses and they tear the home apart.

7. The spirit of marriage destruction: It allows people to get married, but will come and utterly destroy the relationship and will tear them apart.

8. The spirit of anger: It is a very terrible spirit and tears homes apart very rapidly. If you still have the spirit of anger in you, you have to ask God to help you overcome it and you must repent totally. The Bible compares the spirit of anger to the spirit of witchcraft. You must command it to leave.

9. The spirit of Jezebel: It is the spirit that always wants to dominate. When this spirit is upon a woman, her husband would depend on her for every little thing. He cannot take decisions on his own and she commands him and tosses him here and there. Some years ago, we had a case, where a man was jobless and did not bother to look for anything to do. The wife was the one doing everything and would even give him 'pocket money' and clothe him. She built the house they were living in and bought the car they were using. At the end of the year, he would tell his wife that it would not be good for him to go out with her in tattered clothes and she would buy him new ones.

10. Inherited spirits from parents: This usually occurs in polygamous settings. If you notice that your life is taking the negative turn which your mother's life took, or that your husband is treading the path that his father trod, then, you have to cry out to the Lord.

11. Curses: These are curses issued by rivals. If your husband or wife jilted someone to marry you, or there were many of you on the line and you won, the others would not be happy at all. They could say negative words against the marriage and that could actually work against you; especially if the people concerned were cheated or maltreated to favour you.

12. Demonic rites and customs concerning marriage and wedding ceremony: In some cultures, water is poured on the feet of the bride as she is coming into the house of the husband on the night of their wedding. The water could be a concoction or from the queen of the coast. If that was done to you, it might be the source of the problem you are having today.

13. Contaminated wedding rings: Some people dream of their wedding rings being stolen. Some actually get missing for some days only to be found afterwards. They would have been replaced and it is dangerous to put on such wedding rings again.

14. Husbands that are spiritually married to their mothers: I have seen cases of men who saw themselves in the dream being wedded to their mothers. It is a bad sign.

15. Background of polygamy: The spirit of polygamy goes from father to son and daughter in different ways, even in the lives of Christians. Since a Christian cannot have more than one wife at a go, that spirit introduces untimely death at an early stage, so that the person will re-marry; thus recording a second or third spouse for the person. It is more evident in the life of unbelievers, the wife would leave for no reason and the man would be obliged to marry another one, or vice versa.

16. People with familiar or witchcraft spirits: There would always be one problem or the other due to the demands of these spirits in the demonic world. Except the person renounces membership to such associations and goes through serious deliverance, he or she would suffer the exigencies from co-familiar spirits and witches.

17. Satanic deposits: This could come through food or something dropped by an enemy or programmed into the home.

18. Collection of spiritual dowry: This is usually done by occult parents or witches and wizards. They use the virginity of their daughters to get promotion in the spirit world. A victim just finds that she is not interested in men or men avoid her, so that she would remain untouched, because she already has a family spirit husband. Such people need to really pray hard to get delivered.

19. Spirit of incest: This is a serious problem. It is a situation where brother and sister or cousins, uncles and nieces have sexual intercourse. Whether both parties agree to do it or one raped the other, it is a serious problem which affects marriage later on.

20. Demonic attachment to father or mother: This is usually done by parents eating the umbilical cords of their babies. Sometimes, the cord is dried and used as belt and this brings trouble into the life of the child later in life.

One day, during a service, a word of knowledge came forth, that a sister was being hindered by her mother from getting married. The Lord said that if the woman did not release her daughter, she would die within a week. A sister claimed the word and went to her mother and asked her to release her, or else, she would die. The mother asked her what she meant and where she heard that from, and she said it was her pastor that said it. The woman went with her to see the pastor and asked if he was the one that said she would die within a week. The pastor said it was not so, that the Lord gave the word of knowledge and it could be anyone. She then asked her daughter to go out and when she did, she asked the pastor if it was true that the person would die. The pastor confirmed it, since the Lord had said it. The woman revealed that she was afraid that if her daughter got married, she would no longer take care of her that was why she did not want to release her. The pastor assured her that her daughter would continue to look after her even after getting married. Four months after the confession, the sister got someone to marry her.

Many people are still attached to their parents like that. Some have been allowed to get married physically but are still spiritually bound to their parents. Although they are out of their parent's home, they are still spiritually bound by parental chains.

Beloved, after reading through this book, you will agree with me that we are in a warfare. I am confident that God Who made you to read this book will surely work a miracle in your life today as you pray the following prayers. Do not allow the devil to continue to cheat you.

The first thing to do is to examine your life and see where you have fallen short of the glory of God. If there is anything that you have done wrong, confess it to the Lord and ask Him to forgive you. The Bible says that whosoever covers his sins will not prosper; but whosoever confesses and forsakes his sins will receive mercy. Are you seeking God's mercy? Then, identify your faults and confess them to the Lord. Tell the Lord that you do not want to read this book in vain and that the prayer points that you have prayed from it so far, and these ones below will bring revolutionary changes to your home.

Take these prayer points with aggression. Keep firing until victory is sure.

1. Every dead bone in my marital life, receive life, in the name of Jesus.

2. Every strange partner, move away from my home, in the name of Jesus.

3. Every association between my husband (wife) and any strange woman (man), scatter now, in the name of Jesus.

4. Every evil counsel targeted against my marital life, collapse, in the name of Jesus.

5. Every demonic in-law, lose your hold upon my life, in the name of Jesus.

6. Every influence of demonic in-laws upon my marriage, melt away, in the name of Jesus.

7. You spirit husband (wife); lose your hold upon my marriage, in the name of Jesus.

8. Every spiritual material deposited into my womb by spirit husband, come out right now, in the name of Jesus.

9. Every curse upon my childbearing, be cancelled, in the name of Jesus.

10. Every demonic mark in my life contrary to having a settled home, be rubbed off by the Blood of Jesus, in the name of Jesus.

11. Every demonic mark that is anti-marriage in nature, be rubbed off by the Blood of Jesus, in the name of Jesus.

12. Every inherited spirit that is not of God, come out of my life, in the name of Jesus.

13. Every curse issued against my marriage, be broken, in the name of Jesus.

14. Every curse issued against my marital life, break, in the name of Jesus.

15. Every ceremony or ritual done on my wedding day that is working against my life now, be destroyed by the fire of God, in the name of Jesus.

16. Every spiritual dowry collected on my behalf, be returned, in the name of Jesus.

17. Every spiritual marriage between me and my mother (father) be dissolved, in the name of Jesus.

18. Every spiritual marriage between my husband (wife) and his mother (father), be dissolved, in the name of Jesus.

19. Anything that says I will not enjoy my marital life; be roasted, in the name of Jesus.

20. I cancel every negative word that I have pronounced against my marital life, in the name of Jesus.

Other Publications by Dr. D.K. Olukoya

ALL OBTAINABLE AT:

- 322, Herbert Macaulay Street, 2nd Floor, Old First Bank Building, Sabo-Yaba, P.O.Box 12272, Ikeja, Lagos.
- MFM International Bookshop, 13, Olasimbo Street, Onike, Yaba, Lagos.
- IPFY Music Konnections Limited, 48, Opebi Road, Salvation Bus Stop (234-1-4719471,234-8033056093).
- All MFM Church Branches Nationwide and Christian Bookstores.

Safeguarding Your Home

It is no longer news that the home has been under severe attacks. Marriage and the family have been receiving deadly blows from Satan and his angels.

Many people have suffered terribly due to lack of knowledge concerning what it takes to safeguard their homes.

The author has provided a spiritual disinfectant for keeping the home safe and healthy. The prayer points, the biblical teachings and the practical illustrations will show you the steps which you must take in order to make your home enjoy complete immunity from satanic attacks.

About the Author

Dr. D. K. Olukoya is the General Overseer of the Mountain of Fire and Miracles Ministries and The Battle Cry Christian Ministries.

The Mountain of Fire and Miracles Ministries' Headquarters is the largest single Christian congregation in Africa with attendance of over 120,000 in single meetings.

MFM is a full gospel minist   Ghost Fireworks, miracles and the   ver to the uttermost. Absolute hol   d pre- requisite for heaven is open   where your hands are trained to wa

9788021700

Dr. Olukoya holds a first cla   sity of Lagos and a PhD in Mole   Jnited Kingdom. As a researcher, h   t.

Anointed by God, Dr. Olukoya is a prophet, evangelist, teacher and preacher of the Word. His life and that of his wife, Shade and their son Elijah Toluwani are living proofs that all power belongs to God.

ISBN 978-8021-70-0